Georges Franju

MANCHESTER
1824

Manchester University Press

FRENCH FILM DIRECTORS

DIANA HOLMES and ROBERT INGRAM *series editors*
DUDLEY ANDREW *series consultant*

Jean-Jacques Beineix PHIL POWRIE

Luc Besson SUSAN HAYWARD

Bertrand Blier SUE HARRIS

Robert Bresson KEITH READER

Leos Carax GARIN DOWD AND FERGUS DALEY

Claude Chabrol GUY AUSTIN

Claire Denis MARTINE BEUGNET

Marguerite Duras RENATE GÜNTHER

Diane Kurys CARRIE TARR

Patrice Leconte LISA DOWNING

Louis Malle HUGO FREY

Georges Méliès ELIZABETH EZRA

Jean Renoir MARTIN O'SHAUGHNESSY

Coline Serreau BRIGITTE ROLLET

François Truffaut DIANA HOLMES AND ROBERT INGRAM

Agnès Varda ALISON SMITH

FRENCH FILM DIRECTORS

Georges Franju

KATE INCE

Manchester University Press
MANCHESTER AND NEW YORK

distributed exclusively in the USA by Palgrave

Published by Manchester University Press
Oxford Road, Manchester M13 9NR, UK
and Room 400, 175 Fifth Avenue, New York, NY 10010, USA
www.manchesteruniversitypress.co.uk

Distributed exclusively in the USA by
Palgrave, 175 Fifth Avenue, New York, NY 10010, USA

Distributed exclusively in Canada by
UBC Press, University of British Columbia, 2029 West Mall, Vancouver, BC, Canada V6T 1Z2

British Library Cataloguing-in-Publication Data
A catalogue record for this book is available from the British Library

Library of Congress Cataloging-in-Publication Data applied for

ISBN 0 7190 6828 2 *hardback*
EAN 978 0 7190 6828 7

First published 2005

14 13 12 11 10 09 08 07 06 05   10 9 8 7 6 5 4 3 2 1

Typeset in Scala with Meta display
by Koinonia, Manchester
Printed in Great Britain
by Bell & Bain, Glasgow

For Mark Pearson, with thanks

Contents

List of plates

Stills reproduced courtesy of BFI Stills, Posters and Designs. Every effort has been made to trace copyright holders where rights are not attributed.

Series editors' foreword

To an anglophone audience, the combination of the words 'French' and 'cinema' evokes a particular kind of film: elegant and wordy, sexy but serious – an image as dependent on national stereotypes as is that of the crudely commercial Hollywood blockbuster, which is not to say that either image is without foundation. Over the past two decades, this generalised sense of a significant relationship between French identity and film has been explored in scholarly books and articles, and has entered the curriculum at university level and, in Britain, at A level. The study of film as an art-form and (to a lesser extent) as industry, has become a popular and widespread element of French Studies, and French cinema has acquired an important place within Film Studies. Meanwhile, the growth in multi-screen and 'art-house' cinemas, together with the development of the video industry, has led to the greater availability of foreign-language films to an English-speaking audience. Responding to these developments, this series is designed for students and teachers seeking information and accessible but rigorous critical study of French cinema, and for the enthusiastic filmgoer who wants to know more.

The adoption of a director-based approach raises questions about *auteurism*. A series that categorises films not according to period or to genre (for example), but to the person who directed them, runs the risk of espousing a romantic view of film as the product of solitary inspiration. On this model, the critic's role might seem to be that of discovering continuities, revealing a necessarily coherent set of themes and motifs which correspond to the particular genius of the individual. This is not our aim: the *auteur* perspective on film, itself most clearly articulated in France in the early 1950s, will be interrogated in certain volumes of the series, and, throughout, the director will be treated as one highly significant element in a complex process of film production and reception which includes socio-economic and political determinants, the work of a large and highly skilled team of artists and technicians, the mechanisms of production and distribution, and the complex and multiply determined responses of spectators.

The work of some of the directors in the series is already known outside France, that of others is less so – the aim is both to provide informative and original English-language studies of established figures, and to extend the range of French directors known to anglophone students of cinema. We intend the series to contribute to the promotion of the informal and formal study of French films, and to the pleasure of those who watch them.

DIANA HOLMES
ROBERT INGRAM

Acknowledgements

I would particularly like to acknowledge the support of the Arts and Humanities Research Board and the British Academy in bringing this book to completion. During 2002–3, a semester's leave in the AHRB's Research Leave scheme and residence in Paris funded by the British Academy's Small Research Grants competition gave me access to library resources and copies of Franju's films in the Forum des Images, the Bibliothèque du Film, the archives of the CNC, the Cinémathèque française, and the Cinémathèque Royale de Belgique, all of whose staff were always helpful. An initial visit to Paris in 2001 to view films and consult criticism in the BiFi and the Bibliothèque François Mitterand was funded by the University of Birmingham's School of Humanities, and for this I am also grateful. More personally speaking, I thank John Flower, Mike Witt and Graeme Hayes for their initial help with materials, Jean-Pierre Jeancolas, Keith Reader, Phil Powrie, Elizabeth Cowie and Russell Cousins for sharing their knowledge, ideas and enthusiasm about Franju, and Di Holmes and Robert Ingram for being very supportive Series Editors. Papers from draft chapters of the book were delivered at the 20th/21st century French Studies conference in Hartford, Connecticut in April 2002 and the Studies in French Cinema conference in London in April 2003, and my thanks go to the organisers of those events. Material from Chapter 3 was presented in French at one of Jean-Loup Bourget's doctoral seminars at the Ecole Normale Supérieure in January 2003, an opportunity for which I am grateful. My additional thanks go to Gérard Leblanc, who read part of the manuscript in an early draft, and provided valuable interest and encouragement during the most important phase of the project.

Preface

A thematic link exists between this book and my previous one, a study of the performance artist Orlan (*Orlan: Millennial Female*, Oxford and New York, Berg, 2000). As readers who know that book will have noticed, plastic surgery is the medium at the heart of Orlan's most acclaimed series of performances in the early 1990s, and also at the heart of Franju's best-known film, *Les Yeux sans visage*. I have not had cosmetic surgery, and don't anticipate doing so, but if it has fascinated me for this long, it is because it stands in for a trope of self-transformation *and/or* the conferral of identity by others/the Other central to the work of artists from many cultures and periods of history. The idea of writing a book on Franju occurred to me when I first saw *Les Yeux sans visage* at Birmingham's Midland Arts Centre in 1996, a time when work on my Orlan project was well underway.

Note on translations

Where references to published translations are not given, all translations from French are my own.

Introduction

The life of Georges Franju belonged to the cinema. Although he was recognised as an important director as soon as his first significant short, *Le Sang des bêtes*, was shown in Paris in 1948, his reputation as a film-maker has often been and remains eclipsed by the place accorded him in cinema history as the co-founder, with Henri Langlois, of the Cinémathèque française in 1936. In fact, Franju ceased to be closely involved with the Cinémathèque as early as 1938, when he and Langlois divided up the national and international dimensions of the new profession of film archiving so important across Europe in the 1930s, and Franju became the Executive Secretary of the Fédération Internationale des Archives du Film (FIAF), an organisation founded on French initiative (Lebovits and Tranchant 1959: 19). Although he remained in close contact with Langlois throughout the Second World War, became associated with the Cinémathèque again by being appointed an honorary artistic director in the 1980s (Gires 1988: 21), and was writing a script telling the story of the institution at the time of his death (Beylie 1987: 30), Franju always made extremely light of his role in the event for which film history has most often recorded his name. The industry and institutions of cinema were undoubtedly of great importance to him, but films – planning and shooting them and the pleasures afforded by the moving image – were his primary passion.

Franju was born in Fougères, Brittany, on 12 April 1912. Little biographical information about his early life is available in print apart from in one or two anecdotes he often retold about the unforgettable impressions certain images made on him, but before meeting Henri

Langlois in the early 1930s he painted stage sets for the 'Folies Bergères' and 'le Casino de Paris' (Lebovits and Tranchant 1959: 18). Franju and Langlois met via Franju's twin brother Jacques, and together the two cinephiles founded the Cercle du Cinéma, an organisation that screened films and encouraged informal debate about them at each session. In a revealing anticipation of one important tendency of Franju's directorial career, the very first session of the organisation was devoted to horror cinema (18). Many famous names of 1930s Paris attended the Cercle du Cinéma screenings, and the money they raised allowed Langlois and Franju to buy copies of films from dealers and at Paris's flea markets (Maison de la Villette 1992: 51). One important acquisition was the 'Albatros' collection, which included films by Feyder, Epstein, Duvivier, and René Clair, which Franju called a 'collection capitale'[1]; another was the set of films donated by Georges Méliès (88). The Cinémathèque française began with 'un fonds extraordinairement beau et précieux'[2] (88) that was kept in a store Méliès owned at Orly between 1936 and 1938 (Schlockoff 1979: 58). According to Franju, however, the idea of establishing a film-archiving institution came from the reputed film pioneer Germaine Dulac, and almost all the credit for the organisational work of founding it belonged to Dulac, through her connections with Gaumont, to Mme Yvonne Bacheville (later Dornès) for her administrative support, and to Mlle Suzanne Borel (later Mme Georges Bidoult) at the Ministère des affaires étrangères, whose diplomatic representation supplied a grant to the nascent Cinémathèque as it would to FIAF two years later (Schlockoff 1979: 58). Also closely involved with this critical stage in the history of the Cinémathèque was Paul-Auguste Harlé, the director of a review called *La Cinématographie française*, who funded its first purchases and the maintenance of its initial collections (Brumagne 1977: 79). The foundation of the Cinémathèque was a thoroughly collective affair, as Franju's film directing would itself prove to be.

In 1937 Langlois and Franju co-founded a journal that proved far less enduring than the Cinémathèque. Only two issues of *Cinematograph* ever appeared, each in a run of 2000 copies, with 800 of the first issue and 1200 of the second sold (Fieschi and Labarthe 1963: 3). The enterprise foundered because it was not well organised and no

1 'capital collection'.
2 'an extraordinarily fine and precious collection'.

sponsors came forward to keep it going (Brumagne 1977: 82), but not before it published the most important piece of criticism Franju ever wrote, an appreciation of the cinema of Fritz Lang. To Franju's surprise, an issue of the journal reached Lang in Santa Monica, California, and he received a letter of thanks that he clearly treasured (Fieschi and Labarthe 1963: 3). Neither Franju nor Langlois kept a list of the subscribers to *Cinematograph*, but they included names as important as the Prévert brothers, Marc Chagall, and many other painters (Maison de la Villette 1992: 52). According to Georges-Patrick Langlois, the brother and later the biographer of Henri, *Cinematograph* was as much a surrealist review as a cinema journal; it was, in other words, thoroughly impregnated with a spirit of its age that extended well beyond cinema as an art form and an industry (52).

Early in 1940, two years after his appointment as Executive Secretary of FIAF, Franju also co-founded another organisation devoted to the promotion of cinema, the Circuit Cinématographique des Arts et des Sciences. This time his co-founder was not Langlois, but Dominique Johansen, who had also worked for FIAF and whom Franju would later marry (Brumagne 1977: 78). The Circuit Cinématographique des Arts et des Sciences was, like *Cinematograph*, a short-lived initiative, ceasing activity on 31 May 1940 after only a few months, but it was the forerunner of another more significant association, the Académie du Cinéma, founded in 1946, presided over by Georges Auric from 1954 to 1977 and still being run by Dominique Franju at that point (82). After the war Franju became General Secretary of the Institut de Cinématographie Scientifique, a post he held until 1953 and one indicative of an approach to 'the real' that characterised many of the *courts métrages* he made between 1948 and 1958. It is clear that Franju relinquished his series of important executive posts in cinema institutions once he had embarked upon a full-time career as a director, soon after the noted success of his early shorts, and he never returned to this type of work. When Henri Langlois was dismissed from his post at the head of the Cinémathèque early in 1968, an event seen by many as a significant part of the *événements* that would rock France in May of that year and beyond, Franju was not involved in the fracas, although it seems he did sign the petition calling for Langlois to be reinstated. According to one acquaintance and commentator, Franju's appointment as an honorary artistic director of the Cinémathèque not long before his death on

5 November 1987 was 'une distinction qui sembla l'ennuyer pro-
fondément' (Schlockoff 1988: 23).[3]

One way in which Franju renewed his acquaintance with early and
prewar cinema in the 1960s and 1970s was through his collabora-
tions with Jacques Champreux, the grandson of Louis Feuillade and
son of Feuillade's chief operator Maurice Champreux. Franju was still
working with Champreux when he entered his final illness, and the
friendship is a good example of the type of enduring working
relationships that characterised Franju's entire career as a director. In
an interview recorded for Belgian television and radio in 1963, he
contrasted the collaborative character of cinematic work with painting, writing, and composing music, and expressed a clear preference
for collective over solitary work: 'Je déteste tous les métiers où on est
seul. Je n'aime pas être seul. Ce qui est merveilleux dans le cinéma,
c'est qu'on est trente ou quarante' (Vialle 1968: 87).[4] An important
reason why Franju wanted to direct films at all marks a continuity
with his involvement in French cinema's institutions, namely, that
directing is a profession in which one works in a team (Brumagne
1977: 9). In a clearly egalitarian approach to his working practices, he
always called his team 'mes collaborateurs' and not 'mes assistants'
(Maison de la Villette 1992: 130), and his technicians and other crew
members elected to work with him (Vialle 1968: 73). Franju's 'chefs-
opérateurs' included Eugen Shuftan, Marcel Fradetal, Christian
Matras and Henri Decaë, some of the greatest of the period (73), and
his collaboration with the composer Maurice Jarre constitutes the
most significant early part of one of the most distinguished film
music careers of the twentieth century (Jarre went on to work for
David Lean, and composed the scores for *Doctor Zhivago*, *Lawrence of
Arabia* and numerous later big Hollywood productions). Franju met
Jarre when the latter was already working at Jean Vilar's Théâtre
national populaire, and when Jarre played him the composition he
had scored for an Apollinaire poem and had Vilar listen to not long
before, Franju engaged him instantly. Jarre's first score for Franju
was for *Hôtel des Invalides* in 1951 (Brumagne 1977: 55), and the
collaboration lasted until 1963, although Franju also worked with

3 'a distinction by which he seemed profoundly bored'.
4 'I detest all professions that involve working alone. I don't like being alone.
What is marvellous about cinema is that there are thirty or forty of you.'

other distinguished film composers such as Joseph Kosma, Georges Delerue, Georges Van Parys and Georges Auric during these years and subsequently.

Despite his stated and proven preference for collective over solitary work, Franju's attitude on the set was reserved: he never entertained the idea of acting, and did not even like being in the photographs of the shoot required for publicity purposes (Maison de la Villette 1992: 92). The personal qualities his collaborators consistently praised in him were kindness, generosity, and loyalty to his friends, and the professional skills they most often noted were care, meticulousness and a remarkable memory (Vialle 1968: 166). Although he could be truculent and often used blunt and colourful language, everyone who knew him seemed impressed by his honesty, candour, and his complete lack of pretention and snobbery (165). Despite warm praise from his co-workers, however, important misapprehensions about Franju's character and politics did occur, up to and including the extended interview conducted by François Truffaut for *Cahiers du cinéma* in 1959, after the completion of his first two *longs métrages*. Truffaut's semi-affectionate description of Franju as 'Georges le Pessimiste' in his introduction to this interview was based on a remark Franju had made previously about being an 'active pessimist', and was arguably justified by the seriousness of his best-known shorts, the bleak storyline of *La Tête contre les murs*, and *Les Yeux sans visage*'s quietly chilling mode of horror. But Truffaut followed this with a claim that Franju was an anarchist, both a leftist one ('anarchiste de gauche') through his affinity with Buñuel and Vigo, and a rightist one ('anarchiste de droite') through what Truffaut called a 'family likeness' with the writer Céline (Truffaut 1959: 2). Although Buñuel and Vigo were film-makers with whom Franju was happy to recognise an affinity, a connection with Céline has not been made by any other commentator on his work, and implies a misunderstanding on Truffaut's part of Franju's political inclinations and of his relationship with his subject-matter.[5] Early commentaries on the brutality of

5 A similar misunderstanding occurred in the British reception of Franju's 1950s films described by Alan Lovell, which 'too often regarded [him] simply as a director of social exposés' (1962: 8). Despite terming him an anarchist in the title of his pamphlet, Lovell gives a nuanced appreciation of Franju's politics, noting that he is no 'conventional progressive', and that his work makes no programmatically consistent statement about society (8).

Le Sang des bêtes's abattoirs and the virulent anti-war sentiments of *Hôtel des Invalides* had seen Franju labelled as 'féroce' and 'sadique',[6] but the intervention of critics such as Freddy Buache, usually writing in *Positif*, began to establish the necessary distinction between the violence it was Franju's talent to be able to see and film, and any association of violence with his character. The claim of anarchism was one Franju had himself already rebutted in an interview with Buache for *Positif* in 1957, indicating that the dispute over him was ongoing, one element in the rivalry between *Positif* and *Cahiers du cinéma* active at the time. As might be expected, Franju's rebuttal alluded to the preference for collectivities over the individual already described: 'Je suis plutôt même le contraire d'un anarchisme car j'ai horreur de tout ce qui est individuel à partir du moment où il faut des mouvements collectifs' (Buache 1957: 18).[7] As François Chevassu would note much later, the first 'contresens' of Franju was to make of him 'un cinéaste de la cruauté' (Chevassu 1988: 68).[8]

If Franju's place in film history has never been well understood, this is for three main reasons. The first is the limited critical literature on him available: although a lot of material is scattered throughout French and anglophone film journals, the only books published on him since Raymond Durgnat's *Franju* (1967) and Gabriel Vialle's *Georges Franju* (1968), the first two, have been Marie-Madeleine Brumagne's volume of interviews *Georges Franju. Impressions et aveux* (1977), Freddy Buache's *Georges Franju: poésie et vérité* (1996), partly reprinted from 1959, and Gérard Leblanc's *Une esthétique de la déstabilisation* (1992). Most of these writings have only ever been accessible in specialist film libraries. The second reason for Franju's critical obscurity is that an important – arguably the more important – part of his output was in *court métrage*, a format that has always had to struggle for its survival, and cannot count on initial or regular distribution to cinemas, let alone the television screenings and transfer to video and DVD on which the film market has come to depend since the 1980s. The first chapter of this book provides a detailed examination of the production context of Franju's *courts métrages*, and I have listed the most useful books and journal articles

6 'ferocious' and 'a sadist'.

7 'What I really stand for is even the opposite of anarchism, because I abhor all that is individual whenever collective movements can be seen to be necessary'.

8 'misinterpretation'; 'a film-maker of cruelty'.

available on him in in my annotated Select Bibliography. The third reason why Franju's place in film history has been unjustly neglected is that his relationship to it is displaced, or 'out of sync'. I am referring here partly to his links with the surrealist movement, which I discuss at some length in Chapter 3, but particularly to the coincidence of the period when he was directing *longs métrages* with the *nouvelle vague* (Franju's first feature *La Tête contre les murs* was released in Paris in March 1959) and 1960s 'auteur' cinema.

As Claire Clouzot points out in her study of French cinema since the *nouvelle vague*, Franju's filmic style is generally understood as heavily influenced by his predecessors, 'un réalisme fantastique poignant hérité du Surréalisme, du cinéma scientifique de Jean Painlevé et influencé par l'expressionisme de Murnau et de Lang' (Clouzot 1972: 134).[9] These influences root Franju firmly in his cinematic past, and set him apart from the *nouvelle vague*, as Vialle also observes (Vialle 1968: 60). On more than one occasion Franju defended the 'cinéma de Qualité' against which Truffaut and the other *Cahiers du cinéma* directors rebelled, in particular by affirming that studios had given cinema a certain 'mystique' it had lost by being taken into the street. 'Comme beaucoup, je suis partisan du décor naturel, mais ma réflexion, ici, ne concerne pas les films mais *le cinéma* et il est évident que les tournages sur la voie publique ont porté un coup fatal au prestige d'un art dont les murs des studios protégaient, en même temps que les initiés, les secrets de leurs cérémonies' (Brumagne 1977: 70).[10] Neither did he share the enthusiasm of the main *nouvelle vague* directors for improvisation on the set: although inspiration had its place, it had to come in good time, as his films were always fully 'written' before shooting began, at the typewriter (Buache 1957: 21).[11] In Franju's view the *nouvelle vague* was a movement without substance,

9 'a poignant fantastic realism inherited from surrealism and Jean Painlevé's scientific cinema, and influenced by the expressionism of Murnau and Lang'.
10 'I am in favour of shooting outdoors like many people, but what I'm thinking of here is not films themselves but the institution of cinema. It's obvious that location shooting struck a fatal blow to the prestige of an art whose secrets and rituals, as well as its initiates, were protected by studio walls'.
11 Despite expressing a distaste for improvisation, Franju expressed immense admiration for Godard's improvisatory talent. Godard exasperated and excited him in equal measure because he seemed to *need* no one else to make his films, 'C'est Godard et Godard tout seul!' (It's just Godard, on his own!) (Carbonnier and Collombat 1986: 8).

little more than 'un "remous" publicitaire'[12] created by certain directors in favour of their own films, and mounted with the aid of journalists whose job it was to 'discover' new values (Vialle 1968: 92). A real 'wave', according to Franju, had to be international, have a social dimension, and endure (92), and while German expressionism and Italian neo-realism met these criteria, the *nouvelle vague* did not. The French cinema movement he did unhesitatingly qualify as a 'wave' was the cinema of the late 1930s that came in the wake of the Popular Front of 1936. Nobody had dared call the combined cinemas of Carné, Renoir, Duvivier, Feyder and Clair the 'Ecole du Front populaire',[13] but in Franju's opinion the years 1936 to 1938 marked the richest artistic period French cinema had ever seen (Vialle 1968: 91).

Franju, then, remained unimpressed by the excitement generated by the *nouvelle vague*, and aloof from its whole atmosphere. To interviewers pressing him in later years on issues such as the merits of original story-writing, called for and fêted by Truffaut in particular, he responded simply 'je n'ai pas le don d'inventer des histoires' (Brumagne 1977: 69).[14] He had no illusions about being a scriptwriter or ambitions to be one; for Franju the script was just a necessary basic element of the finished film, whose real originality lay in the crafting of its images. As François Chevassu summarises, 'Ce n'est pas dans l'écriture qu'il se revendique créateur, mais dans ce qu'il appelait la "mise en forme", qui était pour lui la seule marque réelle de l'auteur cinématographique' (Chevassu 1988: 69).[15] Franju's views about the *nouvelle vague* tell us volumes about the sense in which he was an *auteur*: as Chevassu states, his films have a personal ethic and aesthetic that is conveyed as clearly in his literary adaptations as in his more obviously 'signature' films (69). We can conclude from these questions of signature that the kind of *auteur* Franju is differs in vital respects from the 'politique des auteurs' formulated by *Cahiers du cinéma* in the 1950s and developed into 'the auteur theory' by Andrew Sarris in the 1960s. Franju himself said that his career was far from exemplary; he never served as assistant to another director, and did very little first-hand observation of other film-makers at work

---

12 'a publicity "stir"'.
13 'the Popular Front school'.
14 'I don't have the story-writing gift'.
15 'He claimed creativity not in writing, but in what he called "putting-into-form", for him the only real mark of the *auteur*.'

(Carbonnier and Collombat 1986: 8). Most of his *courts métrages* were state-funded 'films de commande', or commissions, and in his view his feature films could be looked on in the same way, since 'je n'ai jamais sollicité de producteur. J'ai attendu qu'on me propose des films, et tout s'est enchaîné' (8).[16] As Pierre Gaudin perceptively remarks, the singularity of Franju's work is that it allows the relationship between a 'cinéma d'auteur' and the 'cinéma de commande' to be explored (Maison de la Villette 1992: 11).

Because he has always been received as an *auteur*–stylist – without the links between his deserved reputation as a 'film poet', *auteur* theory and the timing of his contribution to French film being interrogated – Franju's displaced relationship to film history has become something of an enigma. There were not many film poets in Franju's generation of French cinema – in Claude Beylie's words, perhaps just Alain Resnais and 'Jacques Demy dans un autre registre' (Maison de la Villette 1992: 44).[17] But although it has been convenient for French film historians that Franju can stand in for this tradition at the time of the *nouvelle vague*, it has not been so convenient for Franju. The task of opening up the Franju enigma is the one I set myself when I decided to write this book, and in order to undertake it I have organised my enquiry into four chapters. The first chapter, as already stated, examines the production context of Franju's *courts métrages* and offers readings of thirteen of these shorts that group them by theme, rather than chronologically. Chapter 2, the longest of the four, comprises preliminary readings of all the *longs métrages* through the prism of the issue of genre, an approach that has never been applied to most of them. My third chapter tackles the area to which the bulk of existing studies of Franju are limited, his cinematic aesthetics, although it attempts both a new synthesis and an expansion of this field of study. And finally, Chapter 4 investigates gender identities, the structure of the family, and sexualities in Franju's cinema, an area of film criticism that hardly existed when the first books on him were written in the late 1960s, but which is now an indispensable part of the theoretical study of French cinema in its cultural context, that is to say, of most anglophone writing on French film.

16 'I have never sought out a producer. I've waited for films to be offered to me, and
    things have gone from there'.
17 'in another register, Jacques Demy'.

References

Beylie, Claude (1987), 'Tombeau de Georges Franju', *Cinéma* 415 (November), 30.

Brumagne, Marie-Madeleine (1977), *Georges Franju. Impressions et aveux*, Lausanne, l'Age d'Homme.

Buache, Freddy (1957), 'Entretien avec Georges Franju', *Positif* 25–6 (autumn), 13–21.

Carbonnier, Alain and Collombat, Boris (1986), 'Franju ou le fantastique au quotidien', *Cinéma* 369 (24–30 September), 8.

Chevassu, François (1988), 'Franju l'insolite', *La Revue du cinéma* 434 (January), 67–77.

Clouzot, Claire (1972), *Le Cinéma français depuis la nouvelle vague*, Paris, Fernand Nathan – Alliance Française.

Fieschi, Jean-André and Labarthe, André S. (1963), 'Nouvel entretien avec Georges Franju', *Cahiers du cinéma* 149 (November), 1–17.

Gires, Pierre (1988), 'Georges Franju et les yeux d'Edith', *L'Ecran fantastique* 88 (January), 20–1.

Lebovits, Jean-Marc and Tranchant, François (1959), 'Entretien avec Georges Franju cinéaste et poète du merveilleux quotidien', *Cinéma* 34 (March), 16–25.

Lovell, Alan (1962), *Anarchist Cinema*, London, Peace News (Goodwin Press),

Maison de la Villette (1992), *Georges Franju cinéaste*, Paris, Maison de la Villette.

Schlockoff, Alain (1979), 'Entretien avec Georges Franju', *L'Ecran fantastique* 11, 58–70.

Schlockoff, Alain (1988), 'Georges Franju, Souvenirs...', *L'Ecran fantastique* 88 (January), 22–3.

Truffaut, François (1959), 'Entretien avec Georges Franju', *Cahiers du cinéma* 101 (November), 1–15.

1

Documenting modernity: Franju's cinema in the age of the *court métrage*

Franju's place in French film history is inseparable from the shape of his career, a long 'apprenticeship' in short films that preceded the eight features he made between 1958 and 1973. However, to put his late start (aged 46) in *long métrage* down to some delayed blossoming of artistic maturity would be both naïve and uninformed: Franju was already an acclaimed director by the time he moved from the short into the longer film, and as with another prominent postwar director Alain Resnais, the lengthy period for which he continued to make *courts métrages* and the timing of his move into feature film were determined to a considerable extent by economic, legal and political factors. Franju's 'apprenticeship' in *court métrage* is in reality no such thing, as his early short films are among the best he made.

Following the foundation of the Fifth Republic, 1958 saw the establishment in France's governmental apparatus for the first time of a Ministry of Cultural Affairs, with André Malraux as its acclaimed first minister. Up to this point, state policy on cinema had been the responsibility of departments of industry and trade, for whose civil servants and ministers it was inevitably well down the agenda. The institution of a Ministry of Culture in 1958 shortly preceded the start, in 1959, of a funding system that French cinema still enjoys today, the 'avance sur recettes', or policy of granting interest-free loans to first-time directors of feature films that only have to be repaid if the film makes a profit (Forbes 1992: 6). This shift in legislation was instrumental in assisting large numbers of young and untried directors in the making of their first *long métrage* at the end of the 1950s and in the early 1960s, and therefore also in supporting the careers of the central figures of the *nouvelle vague* (Louis Malle and Claude Chabrol had in fact already made their first features; Truffaut's *Les Quatre Cent Coups* and Godard's *A bout de souffle* were both released in 1959). The introduction of the 'avance sur recettes' and the onset of the *nouvelle vague* marked a major shift in the climate French cinema had found itself in for most of the 1950s, but I shall argue here that this climate does not correspond to dominant interpretations of it. Following the postwar reconstruction of the French cinema industry in the late 1940s (film production had returned to prewar levels by 1949 (Jeancolas 2000: 15)), the 1950s are often regarded as tedious and uneventful years in which predictable 'Quality' productions were dutifully churned out and original subject matter, if not directorial talent, was in scarce supply.[1] In a revision of this interpretation, I shall outline how the 1950s were a decade in which cinema's dual identity as art and industry was particularly hotly debated. Rather than stagnant years, they were years of considerable strife and disagreement about what role cinema should have in French national life, about how film-making should be funded, and about the nature and quality of the film production encouraged by different funding systems. If one looks only at *long métrage* production, the artistic predictability and emptiness of the prehistory of the *nouvelle vague* has to be admitted. But by looking at the short film and its 'golden age' in the mid 1950s (Vigo and Breton 1994), a different picture emerges – one of varied and dynamic film-making of high artistic quality. The problem, in sum, is one of exclusive versus inclusive histories: if the rich heritage of *courts métrages* from the period is included in an overview of 1950s French cinema, which has not usually been the case,[2] the 1950s emerge anew as a period in which artistic directing and interesting subject-matter underwent an unusual displacement from feature films to *courts métrages*.

1 See Anon 1957.
2 A particularly striking example of the mutual exclusivity of the histories of *long* and *court métrage* is the review of the state of French cinema conducted by *Cahiers du cinéma* 71 (May 1957). No mention of *court métrage* whatsoever is made in the round table '6 personnages en quête d'auteurs', despite the fact that two of its contributors, Pierre Kast and Roger Leenhardt, are among France's leading directors of short film. A separate review of *court métrage* conducted by Jacques Doniol-Valcroze in the same issue is pessimistically entitled 'Problèmes du court métrage', and takes an astonishingly negative view of the French contribution to the format, in view of the quality and interest of films recently made.

Franju made thirteen of his fourteen shorts during the 'long' decade from 1946 to 1958, and I shall start by tracing how *court métrage* production worked during these years. My readings of the thirteen short films he acknowledged will be grouped thematically rather than chronologically in the second, longer part of the chapter (I shall not discuss *Navigation marchande*, the one documentary he renounced, revealingly, because he had not been allowed full artistic licence as director).

Before addressing *court métrage* at all, however, questions of definition have to be broached: what are the differences between documentary and *court métrage*? The majority of Franju's short films are documentaries about places, institutions and professions of 1950s France, but two of them take the form of summary biographies of great French men and women (George Méliès, and Pierre and Marie Curie), and three of them – *A propos d'une rivière*, *Mon chien* and *La Première Nuit* – contain fictional elements and characters, with fictional elements dominant in *Mon chien* and *La Première Nuit*. Whereas documentary can be given a working definition as 'a record of the real that usually has historical, scientific or educational value', *court métrage* has much broader scope, and can incorporate narrative fiction, biography, fantasy, and theoretically all other genres found in full-length feature films. The only limit to *court métrage* is a technical one – its length, which cannot exceed 1300 metres of film (in 35mm), or 47 minutes (Porcile 1965: 13).[3] This definition was arrived at for the purposes of exhibition – what could be fitted into a programme alongside a full-length feature. It covers everything from the very short advertising 'spot' to narrative films of well over half an hour that are sometimes understandably labelled *moyens métrages*.

As Porcile sets out in his *Défense du court métrage français*, in prewar France cinema programmes consisted of two *longs métrages*. With the exhibition of short films blocked by law, there was clearly no market for their distribution. A law passed on 26 October 1940 decreed that all cinema programmes should consist of one short and one long film, thus creating for the first time a degree of commercial incentive for *court métrage* film-makers. This so-called 'loi d'aide' also introduced a system whereby 3 per cent of the total receipts of the

3 This meterage applied until May 1964, when it was raised to 1600 metres – a good illustration of the arbitrariness of the definitions at issue here (Porcile 1965: 13).

programmes were ploughed back into production of *courts métrages* (Porcile 1965: 17). Views of the interest and quality of short film production under the Occupation differ considerably: whereas the director René Lucot remembers 1941–42 as 'la grande époque du court métrage',[4] with the absence of American imports allowing a celebration of French national culture (Vigo and Breton 1994: 33), other sources emphasise the quantity of promotional and tourist-oriented shorts that were screened, paid for by the sponsors of the main feature and preferred by cinema managers because they incurred no additional expense (25). According to Porcile, the period from 1940 to 1953 certainly marked a considerable increase in *court métrage* production, but it led to 'le règne du n'importe quoi',[5] in which the short film was a product rather than 'une forme véritable de l'expression cinématographique' (Porcile 1965: 18).[6] One noteworthy event of the Occupation period was the organisation of the first *Congrès du film documentaire des Champs-Elysées* in Paris in 1943 (Vigo and Breton 1994: 33).

Immediately after the Liberation circumstances were extremely difficult for film-makers of all kinds: little film stock was available, there were often power cuts, and studios were closed if they were not destroyed (Jeancolas 2000: 14). The setting up of the Centre National de la Cinématographie (CNC) in 1946 was the first major step in the rebuilding of an ethos of creation that was well underway by the end of the 1940s, although it was not a measure that emerged entirely out of the blue: the establishment of support structures that would protect French cinematic production from unfettered international economic competition had been mooted in the 1930s, and rumours about the possibility of nationalising the cinema circulated throughout 1945 (14). Although founded as early as 1946, the CNC did not acquire the personnel and the structures to become an effective body for several years. Film production itself, meanwhile, was boosted by the renewal and extension of the 1940 'loi d'aide' on 29 September 1948.

These were the circumstances in which Franju planned the shooting schedule of *Le Sang des bêtes*. As with most of the acclaimed documentaries made in France between the Liberation and the early 1950s, the support and financial assistance of some well-placed and

4 'the great era of the short film'.
5 'the reign of "anything goes"'.
6 'a true form of cinematographic expression'.

cinephile individuals were vital to the realisation of the film project: the producer of *Le Sang des bêtes* was Paul Legros, whose company Forces et Voix de France would also finance Franju's next two films. Legros funded *Le Sang des bêtes* despite the problems of distribution and risk of censorship likely to be run by the unabashed depiction of multiple acts of animal slaughter. Franju was introduced to Legros by a figure vital to the rising fortunes of *court métrage* cinema in postwar France, Jacques Chausserie-Laprée, director of the CNC's 'service du court métrage'. In Franju's words, 'C'est à Chausserie-Laprée que l'école documentaire française doit son existence et ce rayonnement incomparable dont les cinémathèques du monde gardent les témoignages' (Brumagne 1977: 20).[7]

By the early 1950s the issue of the artistic merit of the growing number of *courts métrages* was being urgently debated by many involved in the cinema industry. Many emerging and would-be directors favoured a change from the undiscriminating 'loi d'aide' to a funding mechanism that rewarded quality, while distributors and some producers wanted a return to the double programming of feature films that had prevailed until 1940 (Vigo and Breton 1994: 26). Under pressure from both lobbies, two government decrees were passed that attempted to please everyone: on 6 August 1953 aid calculated on a percentage of receipts was abolished in favour of 'primes à la qualité',[8] while on 21 August 1953 the obligation cinema managers had been under since 1940 to start every programme with a *court métrage* of the same nationality as the main feature was also abolished. The double programme was not to be imposed, but it seemed that it would once again be tolerated (Porcile 1965: 18). According to the system of quality premiums, 150 films per year would be pre-selected and viewed by a jury made up of the Director of Cultural Relations, the Director of the CNC, two other ministers or ministers' representatives, three representatives of the Critics' Association, three directors of *courts métrages* and three producers of *courts métrages*. Of these films, 80 would receive the full 'prime' allowed of 1,000,000 old francs, with the rest of the funding distributed among the remaining films as the jury thought fit (Porcile 1965: 19–20). However, neither decree took effect immediately, and a long battle ensued

7 'the French documentary school owes its very existence to Chausserie-Laprée, as well as its incomparable influence, testified to by the world's film archives'.
8 'quality premiums'.

over which system of funding and programming would prevail.

In this bellicose atmosphere a group of *court métrage* makers came together, of which Franju was a founder member. The 'Groupe des trente' (so called despite already numbering 43 by the end of the year) first met on 26 October 1953, and on 20 December issued the 'Déclaration du Groupe des trente' (Vigo and Breton 1994: 26). This called for the repeal of the decree that allowed a return to the double programme, and took up a firm stance behind funding based on quality, drawing attention to the international pre-eminence French short films had recently acquired:

> L'école française du Court-Métrage se distingue par son style, par sa tenue, par l'ambition de ses sujets. Les Courts-Métrages français ont souvent rencontré la faveur du public. Ils circulent dans le monde entier. Il n'est pas un festival international où ils ne se taillent pas une large place, presque toujours la première. (Vigo and Breton 1994: 40)[9]

The 'Groupe des trente' was opposed by the 'Association des producteurs indépendants et réalisateurs des courts-métrages', created in February 1954 and presided over by Louis Cuny, which argued against the 'Groupe des trente' that no committee or commission such as the proposed jury could assume the right to judge what 'quality' was, and that popularity with the cinema-going public should be the only measure of which films should be funded. Consistently with this position, the association wanted a straightforward return to aid for *courts métrages* based on a percentage of receipts (Vigo and Breton 1994: 26). There were many months of dispute before this situation was finally resolved in favour of the 'Groupe des trente', but by March 1955 quality premiums were instituted, and the law allowing a return to the double programme was finally buried. A supplementary regulation introduced by the CNC on 1 July 1955 meant that at least one of the films in a programme including one or more short films before the main feature had to be French (Porcile 1965: 27–8): in other words, if the feature film was not French, one short had to be. Funding for *courts métrages* made in France finally seemed secure,

9 'The French *court métrage* school is distinguished by its style, its success, and by the ambition of its subjects. French short films have often met with the approval of their audiences. They are distributed world wide. There is no international festival at which they do not win themselves a large place, almost always in the highest rank.'

and organised to ensure quality film-making. By 5 April 1956 the 'Groupe des trente' could already note a progression in the quality and quantity of short films, and published a statement to this effect (Vigo and Breton 1994: 41).

The climate in which Franju's shorts from *A propos d'une rivière* onward were made was thus a secure one. Jacques Floud, appointed Director of the CNC in 1952 when Jacques Chausserie-Laprée was still in charge of its *court métrage* service, recalls the five-year period from 1954 to 1958 as being the true 'âge d'or' of the short film (Vigo and Breton 1994: 28): on average, over 300 shorts a year were produced during these years (Porcile 1965: 29). Floud himself was a champion of *court métrage* through being in favour of encouraging all forms of frustrated talent to break through, and established directors such as René Clair and Julien Duvivier considered him their tormentor (Vigo and Breton 1994: 28). Despite a considerable amount of campaigning, the profile of *court métrage* remained low throughout the 1950s, since shorts were never mentioned on posters or other pre-distributed advertising. They continued to suffer under the unfortunate and uninformative labels of the 'première partie' and the 'complément de programme' (Porcile 1965: 13).

After 1956 the 'Groupe des trente' multiplied its initiatives to increase the public's knowledge and appreciation of *court métrage*. Exchange visits with Czechoslovakia and the USSR were set up in which directors representing their national film industry travelled to the host country with a week's screenings of recent short films (Vigo and Breton 1994: 26–7). From 1955 onwards Tours hosted the 'Journées internationales du film de court métrage' that continued throughout the 1950s and 1960s, a precursor to today's annual short film festival at Clermont Ferrand (26–7). In 1959 came the introduction of the 'avance sur recettes', more lasting in its effects than the laws of either 1940 or 1953, since it coincided with the start of the *nouvelle vague* and would remain a force for the rest of the century. It suddenly became possible for inexperienced directors to make the feature films they had been wanting to make: the 'avance sur recettes' supported the cinema of 'auteurs' which the critics of *Cahiers du cinéma* had been calling for to replace the Quality superproductions that had dominated French cinema during the 1950s.[10] For *court*

---

10 Anon 1957; Dorsday 1952; Truffaut 1954.

métrage, however, the picture was less rosy. Many of the members of the 'Groupe des trente' (which by the end of the 1950s numbered at least three times 30 directors) either took advantage of the new opportunities in *long métrage* or transferred their labour and energies to television, which was expanding rapidly at this juncture (Vigo and Breton 1994: 27). The impact of the 'avance sur recettes' system on *court métrage* making was indirect and took a year or two to register, but it was undoubtedly negative, as both Jacques Floud and Jean-Pierre Jeancolas observe (28, 40). Directors such as Franju and Alain Resnais were never to return to the short film.

The decade between the postwar reconstruction of French cinema and 1959 was, then, a unique period in the history of French *court métrage*. This quantity and quality of film production stood out from earlier or later decades because of the legal and economic measures I have outlined, but the distinction of what became known as the *école française du court métrage*, whose intellectual centre was the 'Groupe des trente', was also artistic (its film-makers were inspired by the great documentaries made by Luis Buñuel, Robert Flaherty and the British Griersonian school in the 1930s and 1940s), and politico-cultural. In this instance 'politico-cultural' refers to the particular character of French cultural politics under the Fourth Republic, whose administrations both oversaw and contributed to fostering a concentrated period of modernisation and technologisation. Social change in France had perhaps never been so rapid or so dynamic as it was during these years: everyday and working lives were transformed by a wave of modernising industrialisation comparable to American Fordism of the 1920s, by the onset of a consumer culture that revolutionised the nature and rhythms of domestic existence, and by the shifting demographic patterns caused by decolonisation and the immigration that accompanied it. Aspects of these successive waves of social change were taking place on a similar scale in other Western nations during the same period, but it has been argued that France was affected later and over a shorter period than other countries, meaning that change was more acute, more concentrated (Ross 1995).

Documentary cinema was a privileged cultural form for the recording of this social and industrial modernisation, and one actively supported by state funding. A considerable proportion of documentary output in the late 1940s and 1950s was, therefore, effectively conceived, shot and distributed as cultural propaganda. Franju's films about George Méliès and Pierre and Marie Curie and the many comparable biographical *courts métrages*[11] can be seen as cultural propaganda responding to and competing with the biopics about the lives of great (American and non-American) scientists and artists made by the Hollywood studios in the postwar years. Françoise Rossi's review of documentaries that took agricultural practices as their subject makes a good example of how the cultural propaganda of state-commissioned film was an integral element of the cinema industry at this time (Maison de la Villette 1992: 150–5). France's Ministry of Agriculture had in fact commissioned hundreds of educational films before the Second World War, but technicians and agricultural engineers working with a professional cameraman made most of these. To ensure that the films did get viewed, the Ministry lent them to agricultural communities for free and subsidised the cost of the projection equipment (150). The work of professional film directors such as Jean Benoit Lévy on films such as *Peau de pêche* and *La Source* in the 1930s opened the door for directors such as Georges Rouquier, Franju, and Dimitri Kirsanoff in the postwar period, for whom commissioned documentary projects were 'la forme idéale d'expression' (151),[12] rather than a second string to their career – a situation also applying for many of the directors in the 'Groupe des trente'. These documentaries both treated a subject – rural life – otherwise marginalised in French cinema and brought to that treatment a real 'écriture cinématographique', not the sensationalising or reductive approach of much television reportage. The filmic style of Kirsanoff's *Faits divers à Paris* (1948) has seen it hailed as a genuinely neo-realist French film (151).

It is of course questionable whether much of the cinematic cultural propaganda contained in postwar French *courts métrages* ever reached the audiences for whom it was intended – whether it was able to exercise the influence that a definition as propaganda really requires. When asked if films such as his *En passant par la Lorraine* and *Les Poussières* really had this kind of influence, Franju replied 'On peut se demander sur quoi, sur qui et dans quel sens?' (Brumagne 1977: 25).[13]

11 For example Resnais's *Van Gogh* and *Gauguin*, Yannick Bellon's *Colette*, Marc Allégret's *Avec André Gide*, Jean Mitry's *Images pour Debussy*, Paul Paviot's *Lumière*. See Gauthier 1995 and Porcile 1965 for further examples.
12 'the ideal form of expression'.
13 'We may ask on what, on whom, and in what sense?'

What is certain is that the flourishing of *court métrage* in 1950s France proves that the limitation apparently imposed by working to a 'commande' – the reduction of artistic freedom entailed in not being able to choose one's subject – may not be a limitation at all. Another kind of freedom is possible, as Alain Resnais confirms: 'Si, à partir de la commande, on a toute liberté, c'est l'idéal' (Vigo and Breton 1994: 32).[14] In Franju's cinema as in Resnais's, this freedom is evident in the way in which a style and a stance are imprinted upon the predetermined subject.

French feature films of the 1950s were roundly criticised, especially by the critics of *Cahiers du cinéma*, for their predictability, lack of imagination, and reliance on production values. They traded on the reputations of familiar stars and directors, and on a dubious quality ensured by improved funding, especially from 1954 onwards. With a few honourable exceptions listed by François Truffaut in his 1954 article 'Une certaine tendance du cinéma français' – Jean Renoir, Robert Bresson, Jean Cocteau, Max Ophuls, Jacques Tati – French cinema was devoid of originality and interesting subjects, and dominated by historical dramas and literary adapations that depended only on appropriate source material and efficient scriptwriters. The younger generation of cinephiles saw not a single director of *long métrage* with whom it could identify.[15] But as conducted by the critics of *Cahiers du cinéma* at least, the project of encouraging and creating a cinema of *auteurs* was blind to the wealth of individualised talent at work within France's *court métrage* industry. By the time they came to direct feature films Franju, Resnais and Marker were undoubtedly generally considered *auteurs*, but questions of how they had acquired this status and how it fitted into the film industry as a whole have been glossed over by historians. In sum, it is certain that much of the directorial talent that emerged at the time of the *nouvelle vague* did not appear from nowhere; it was already at work within the French *école du court métrage*. In the words of Georges Sadoul, 'Quarante neuf nouveaux metteurs en scène entreprirent, en 1960, leur premier film. On

---

14 'To be commissioned and then have complete freedom is the ideal situation'.

15 In Jean-Pierre Jeancolas's words, 'Nous avions autour de vingt ans, nous étions une génération de cinéphiles, et nous ne pouvions voir, dans le long métrage, aucun cinéaste avec lequel nous identifier' ('We were about twenty, we were a generation of cinephiles, and in *long métrage* we could not see a single film-maker we could identify with') (Vigo and Breton 1994: 39).

appela "nouvelle vague" ce mouvement subit ... Cette promotion avait été préparée par l'essor artistique du court métrage, qui eut, après 1950, pour centre le Groupe des trente' (Vigo and Breton 1994: 27).[16]

Fourth Republic France and postwar Paris: documenting a changing nation

No significant publicity for its products was provided by the *court métrage* industry in the 1950s, but short films were widely discussed in *ciné-clubs*, press reviews and film journals. Franju had also become the particular champion of the other leading journal of the decade apart from *Cahiers du cinéma*, *Positif*, which in its May 1956 issue had proclaimed him 'le plus grand cinéaste français' (Demeure and Kyrou 1956). Apparently more kindly disposed than *Cahiers* to *court métrage*, *Positif* had also published two substantial pieces by Freddy Buache on Franju's work, an article early in 1955 and an interview in the autumn of 1957. Franju was, in short, already an acclaimed film-maker by the time he was presented with his first opportunity to direct a feature film in 1958.

The diversity of Franju's thirteen acknowledged *courts métrages* has meant that existing studies, perhaps discouraged by the films' lowly status as state-funded cultural 'propaganda', have treated them as thematically totally eclectic, and therefore individually and in chronological order. In a modification of this approach, and in an attempt to trace patterns of coherence among the films, I shall discuss them in

16 'Forty-nine new directors made their first film in 1960. This sudden movement was called a "new wave" ... This promotion had been prepared by the artistic prominence of the short film, whose centre was the "Groupe des trente" from 1950 on'. Roger Odin differentiates his assessment of the 'Groupe des trente' from this view of Sadoul's, saying 'on ne saurait affirmer, comme on l'a fait parfois, que le Groupe des trente préfigure la Nouvelle Vague. Les deux phénomènes ne nous semblent en rien comparables' ('it cannot be claimed, as it sometimes has been, that the Groupe des trente prefigures the *nouvelle vague*. The two phenomena do not seem remotely comparable') (Odin 1998: 50–1). While Odin is right to point out that the two groupings were fundamentally different (the 'Groupe des trente' was based around a common project explained in the 1953 'Déclaration' and demonstrated in its members' films, while the *nouvelle vague* had no common project, but was a loose association of talented individuals) this does not undermine Sadoul's point about their artistic proximity and human overlap.

groupings derived from those recently proposed by Guy Gauthier to cover the entirety of French documentary during the postwar period. By merging some of the seven headings under which Gauthier lists the principal sub-genres of French documentary in the 1950s (Gauthier 1995: 67–8),[17] the following four areas are arrived at: (1) biographical portraits of great men and women, especially painters, writers, film directors and musicians, (2) the cinema of the 'inaccessible' (nature, the environment, the sea), (3) the cinema of memory, and (4) the cinema of everyday life, particularly working life in industry and agriculture. Of Franju's *courts métrages*, *Le Grand Méliès* and *Monsieur et Madame Curie* fall into the first category, and *A propos d'une rivière* and *Mon chien* into the second, provided that the area of 'nature and the environment' is defined flexibly enough to take in the issue of animal welfare. In Franju's work, the 'cinema of memory', a category of documentary initially derived in part from *Hôtel des Invalides*, applies also to *Notre Dame, cathédrale de Paris*, a document of architectural and human history, and to another film that takes the sites and institutions of Paris as its subject, *Le Sang des bêtes*, because of the way it acts as a memorial to ancient and changing 'quartiers' of the city. The fourth area, the cinema of everyday and working life, is represented in Franju's work primarily by *En passant par la Lorraine* and *Les Poussières*, rather less securely by *Sur le pont d'Avignon*, but also by *Le Sang des bêtes* and *Le Théâtre national populaire*, since the latter documents a very contemporary institution, the thoroughly modern, touring theatre company that was Jean Vilar's Théâtre national populaire (TNP) in the 1950s. Between them the four areas account for eleven films, leaving two which cannot comfortably be accommodated: the prewar silent *Le Métro*, and the primarily fictional *La Première Nuit*, Franju's first and last *court métrage* respectively. The Paris Métro provides the setting and an implicit documentary-style theme of *La Première Nuit*, and links the two films, which are on this count candidates for a fifth group of 'Paris' films that overlaps areas (1), (3) and (4), particularly (3).

---

17 Excluded from this list and Gauthier's seven categories are the ethnographic and sociological films that grew up around Jean Rouch's 'Comité du film ethnographique', created in 1952 (Gauthier 1995: 69).

Lives of the famous

Le Grand Méliès and *Monsieur et Madame Curie* are most conveniently labelled homages to a pioneer of cinema and to France's most famous scientific couple respectively, and thus as biographical. Since both films treat figures long dead at the moment they were made, however, they are necessarily reconstructed biographies in which actors play Georges Méliès and Pierre and Marie Curie. For *Le Grand Méliès* Franju turned his acquaintance with the Méliès family (Brumagne 1977: 27; Vialle 1968: 61 n38[18]) to account by having early cinema's great fantasist played by his son, André Méliès, and by so constructing his film that a role is created for Méliès's widow. Mme Méliès appears with her son (as himself at this point) in a prologue to the reconstructed selection of events from her husband's life that constitute the biography proper, and again in a kind of epilogue, emerging from the Métro opposite Père-Lachaise cemetery to take flowers to Georges's grave. The involvement of the Méliès family in the film is furthered by having the commentary to these two sections of the film read by Méliès's granddaughter. This excursus to 1953 (the present of the film) forms a frame that sets the film's sad and nostalgic tone, since it introduces the location of the home for retired humorists at Orly where Méliès died. The central part of the film, narrated by a male voice, comprises a scene at Méliès's toy shop at the Gare Montparnasse in 1928, his magician's stage act at the Théâtre Robert Houdin in the 1890s, the meeting with Louis Lumière at which Lumière refused to sell him his *cinématographe* at any price, Méliès's early experiments with his own cinecameras, his enormous success and fame at the height of his career, and the sad downfall that followed the failure of his business acumen to match up to his inventive genius (his films were copied and the copies exploited). By including excerpts from some of Méliès's cleverest films and by showing how cinema of the silent era sought audiences at fairs and carnivals (the 'cinema of attractions'), Franju fits a homage to early cinema into his personal tribute to Méliès.

Like *Le Grand Méliès*, *Monsieur et Madame Curie* covers only key moments in the lives of its protagonists, since it focuses on the scientific advance that made Marie Curie famous – the discovery of

18 Franju and Henri Langlois knew and saw Méliès during 1937, and Franju paid for Méliès's last stay in hospital in 1938 (Méliès died on 21 January 1938).

radium, achieved early in her career. The film is the story of a relationship as much of scientific work, and depicts the Curies' marriage and
professional partnership as serene, contented, and tragically cut short
by Pierre's death in an accident in 1906. As in *Le Grand Méliès*, there
is no live dialogue, but a commentary, taken in *Monsieur et Madame
Curie* from Marie Curie's biography of her husband. Two sequences
in the Curies' laboratory and in a barn in the courtyard of the Ecole de
Physique depict Marie's discovery of radium, and a third short final
sequence narrates some contented days *en famille* spent away from
Paris just before Pierre's death. By ending his film on this tragic note
and using Marie's biography of Pierre as its commentary Franju's
emphasis (as the film's title gives away) is on partnership and
collaborative work: Pierre is the 'être admirable' who is rewarded by
being appointed as Professor of Physics at the Institut de France, as
social mores of the early twentieth century dictated, but the Prix Nobel
was awarded to both scientists.

Nature and animals

The fictional elements created by the reconstruction and abbreviation
of biography in *Le Grand Méliès* and *Monsieur et Madame Curie* are
stronger in the two *courts métrages* I am classing as part of the 'cinéma
de l'inaccessible' (both are located out of the city and are to do with
the life and treatment of animals). In *Mon chien*, Pierrot is a large Alsatian
owned by a bourgeois family who are seen leaving Paris for the
grandes vacances after an opening scene in which the little girl of the
family, an only child, plays with Pierrot in the garden to the sound of
piano practice in the neighbourhood. Once out of the city, the car
drives slowly down a woodland track to a secluded spot where Pierrot
is let out, to half-questioning and half-accusing looks from the little
girl. The dog is led a distance through undergrowth by the father, who
removes his collar, orders him 'Couchez!',[19] and dodges furtively back
to the car. Protest and sobs from the little girl, who is dragged forcibly
back from running towards her pet by her mother, are to no avail, and
Pierrot is abandoned at the spot. The rest of the film follows the dog's
attempts to rejoin human society, as he is locked out of a village church

19 'Lie down!'

just entered by a wedding party and spends the entire following twenty-four hours returning home to the Paris suburbs, where he barks in vain outside a locked gate. Taken by the police, Pierrot is transferred to the 'Préfecture de Police Fourrière' (the police pound), where he is caged for the forty-eight hours allowed for in law for owners to claim pets that are genuinely lost. Since he will not be claimed, his fate (one that the commentary reminds us is shared by 4000 dogs each year) is to be gassed or supplied for vivisection: this is the intertextual link between the end of *Mon chien* and *Les Yeux sans visage*, which both feature shots of rows of maltreated and unhappy dogs, barking, whining and whimpering in their cages.

Mon chien is, then, a kind of docu-drama designed to draw attention to the issue of the abandonment of dogs. Franju was a confirmed dog-lover, and the film was a personal project and not a commission.[20] Pierrot the Alsatian is the central character of the film, the only other acted part that merits the term being the little girl that loves her pet (after the dog is led away from his cage at the end of the film, her voice is heard on the soundtrack saying 'Pierrot ... mon Pierrot ... où es-tu parti?'[21]). Franju reflected later that it had been a mistake to include a human character (Fieschi and Labarthe 1963: 9), as it over-sentimentalised the film, which did not measure up to his usually rigorous aesthetic: in order for it to do so, he would have had to film the extermination of the abandoned dogs, and he reflected that he should have done this (Brumagne 1977: 34). By far the most interesting part of the film from a cinematographic point of view is the sequence of shots of caged dogs with which it closes, memorable for its remarkable pathos.

A propos d'une rivière, also made in 1955 but to a commission by the 'Institut national des eaux et des forêts' (part of the Ministry of Agriculture), is considerably truer to the no-holds-barred aesthetic which had contributed to Franju's reputation since *Le Sang des bêtes*, particularly in a shot of a salmon just fished from the water being brutally killed by blows to its head with a large stone. However, the film, often known in the 1950s under its working title *Le Saumon*

20 Claude Beylie recalls Franju in the 1930s living in a tiny fourth floor flat on the quai St-Michel with only his dog Gaston for company (Maison de la Villette 1992: 35).
21 'Pierrot ... my Pierrot ... where have you gone?'

atlantique, also romanticises the practice of salmon-fishing through the fictional framework of an 'enfant-pêcheur'[22] who realises his childhood dream of becoming a fisherman, a device through which Franju is able to juxtapose human and animal life cycles. At the start of the film the boy follows an adult fisherman carrying his tackle down a path next to their local river, spying on him captivated, only to turn back from this vision of adult freedom and skill to return to his own little fish. Later the same day he listens by the fireside, equally captivated, to tales of the river salmon's journey to the sea and epic return upstream to spawn. This narrative is the documentary proper, and after one iris out from the story-telling situation to its start, the image of the old man and the boy by the fire fades out to empty chairs, and the words JE SUIS DEVENU PECHEUR DE SAUMON[23] appear on the screen: the fisherman of the sequences that follow is identified as the yearning child become a man.

Longer than a number of Franju's *courts métrages* at twenty-five minutes, *A propos d'une rivière* goes into absorbing detail about the types of bait used in salmon-fishing – small insects, juicy flies, and when all else fails a whole shrimp – the beauty of the hook itself, made of 'plumes d'oiseaux rares',[24] and the temperament of the fisherman. Steely determination as he sharpens his hook, checks his knots, and wades out into the river to cast his line turns into honed concentration on hooking his prey, shown in close-ups on his hunting eyes, then back into determination as he tells the salmon he will chase it through rivers to the foot of the Pyrenees if necessary. When this particular salmon is hooked, reeled in and killed, the film moves on to document the life cycle of its species, including the sober facts of the number of salmon shot by poachers in spring, their most vulnerable season. The salmon succeed in reproducing despite these 'massacres', but the commentary on their struggles to survive ends on a sombre note, over shots of the darkened Atlantic, 'Et parmi les grands mâles qui tentent de regagner la mer, on dit qu'aucun survit au voyage'.[25]

22 'boy fisherman'.
23 'I BECAME A SALMON FISHERMAN'.
24 'the feathers of rare birds'.
25 'And among the large males that try to get back to the sea, it is said that not one survives the journey'.

Cinema of memory

Hôtel des Invalides, the chief instance in Franju's cinema where he departed from an approach bound to meet with governmental approval, was commissioned by Henri Claudel, cultural relations spokesman and manager of the funding of cultural projects at the Ministère des affaires étrangères. As Franju recounts it, the choice of subject for the film was highly fortuitous: invited into Claudel's office at the Ministry, he was asked to come up there and then with a subject for a 'cultural' documentary to follow *En passant par la Lorraine*. Spotting the dome of the Invalides from Claudel's window, Franju pointed at it and said 'Ça!', to which Claudel replied 'Ah, je vous vois venir avec vos moignons!'.[26] Franju's response was that there would be neither peg-legs nor blood, but that his film would be pacifist (Brumagne 1977: 26; Leblanc 1992: 81). From the first, Franju was going to take the opportunity to voice his pacifism and condemn all war, not at all the same approach as a politicised critique of his country and, by implication, the administration of the time. Henri Claudel proved a stalwart defender of Franju's condemnation of the horrors of war as, like other key proponents of *court métrage* in the early 1950s, Claudel cared more about the making of 'films de prestige' than he did about respecting a pre-established ideology of representation (Leblanc 1992: 79–81). The conflict resulting from the film was internal to departments of state rather than between Franju and his subsidisers, since the film itself had no connection to departments that dealt with the French army, military history, and national defence. A record of this relationship detached from areas of risk appears in the first frame of the film, preceding even the credits, which explains that its 'auteurs' have limited their investigation to the part of the institution formed by the Musée de l'Armée, considering it unnecessary to treat the Hôtel's links to the Ministry of Defence in the same documentary.

Two narrators present and describe the Hôtel, the first historically and architecturally, and the second – the museum guide and a veteran himself – from the point of view of its collections. The guide's tour forms the central part of the film, and is framed by the commentary written by Franju and read by Michel Simon. Two visual motifs link the two halves of this commentary and the film's opening and closing

26 'Aha, I can see you and your peg-legs coming!'

sections: the presence of a couple of lovers amused by some of the weaponry in the Hôtel's courtyards and associated with the troupe of children heard singing as they march away towards the Place des Invalides at the end of the film, and the flocks of sparrows that swirl around the leaden skies overhead. The first motif, in particular, works in counterpoint to the film's dominant subject of war. The guide's commentary, delivered in a high-pitched and rather androgynous if military-style voice, barks recommendations of interest at the usually invisible group of visitors touring the Musée de l'Armée: Franju's camera becomes one of them by moving in their midst, and rarely alights on individual visitors or the guide himself (the only shot confirming the presence of a group films their shadows and then a rear view as they exit the building into an interior courtyard). By incorporating a pre-existing tour into its action *Hôtel des Invalides* is effectively making extensive use of found objects, but shots of the many suits of armour, weaponry, flags and paintings never simply re-frame the views seen by the casual visitor. Dramatic low-angle views of rows of flags and suits of armour mounted on horses reproduce sights seen on the battlefield, as do shots of Napoleon's camp bed, desk, and his horse and faithful dog, stuffed. Shots of the plane flown by Charles Guynemer, one of the ace pilots of the First World War, are accompanied by the sound of airgun fire created by the percussion section of Maurice Jarre's orchestra. The final scene takes place under the dome where the tombs of Napoleon and Marshall Foch are situated, the first a monumental construction in the porphyry used for Roman emperors, the second borne on the shoulders of statues of infantrymen. It is preceded by a scene in the Invalides' chapel of Saint Louis, where thunderous organ music creates a dramatic setting for a mass attended by thirty or so elderly, infirm and disfigured veterans, all of whose uniforms display a variety of medals.

Exterior views of the Hôtel des Invalides and interiors of the exhibits in the Musée de l'Armée already constitute an interesting historical film, but what transforms *Hôtel des Invalides* into a remarkable anti-war document, in addition to camerawork that reproduces the action of combat, are allusions made to the operations of memory through the various means of visual representation included in the film. The notion of reflection (here equalling 'representation') is introduced early, in a perfectly symmetrical shot of the dome of the Invalides reflected in a pool. The re-creation of soldiers' points of view during the tour is supplemented by shots of drawings and paintings in which action is simulated through the movement of the camera; this animation-effect is indulged extensively in the filming of a painting by Edouard Petaille which inspired the famous song 'Le Rêve passe'. Jarre's score orchestrates this song as its words are reproduced in subtitles over various shots of Petaille's and other paintings. Shortly afterwards, the lovers seen in the courtyard at the start of the film come back into view, as the woman comes across a periscope. After seeing a soldier's head in its upper mirror she re-angles it to reflect herself, and checks the state of her hair – a striking juxtaposition with what follows, as the periscope's 'lens' then acts as the projector of newsreel footage of trenches in the First World War. Instead of violent deaths, figures of the catastrophic total French and Allied losses in the Great War are shown on the screen. Franju's inclusion of this variety of visual media in *Hôtel des Invalides* emphasises the prominence in memory's operations of looking, the gaze and visual technologies. A final possible allusion to these (and to the memorial status of Franju's film) occurs in the guide's final instructions to his visitors, 'Tête gauche' to look at Napoleon's tomb, 'Tête droite'[27] to look at Marshall Foch's.

Since he was known for his anti-ecclesiastical views, it surprised some of Franju's contemporaries that he agreed to make *Notre Dame, cathédrale de Paris*, an architectural but also necessarily a historical study of Paris's most important religious edifice. Clerics and worshippers are, however, almost entirely absent from the film, in part because the Ministère des Beaux-Arts asked Franju not to film services or the clergy (Vialle 1968: 172). Instead, he represents cardinals metonymically by their red hats and includes just two shots of nuns, one full shot of two flapping wimples, and one close-up from the back of a nun collecting for the poor, her eyes obscured by her headgear. Directly after this a small congregation comes briefly into view, featuring one young girl in particular (all the worshippers that appear are actors), but the majority of shots of the cathedral's interior are images of unpeopled space in its nave, transept or vaulted heights. Franju makes liberal use of tracking shots that convey this desertion, across the empty upholstered chairs in the cathedral's nave and vertically up to the pointed summits of its gothic arches. One tracking

27 'Eyes left' and 'Eyes right'.

shot moves along a frieze of reliefs of scenes from the life of Christ that seem to be carved of wood, although they glow golden enough to be of bronze. Interspersed with the tracking shots are many fixed shots of decorative objects and features – illuminated statues, a table of votive offerings, a chandelier, stained glass windows, the northern rose window, headstones behind the chevet, and the alarming gargoyles at the east end of the cathedral that Fréderic de Towarnicki's commentary calls 'les guetteurs de Notre Dame'.[28] During the film's closing series of shots the commentary states how Paris has changed so much more than Notre Dame in eight centuries, a reminder of the dynamism and popular basis of history that is also the subject of the film's epigraph, by the modernist architect Le Corbusier, 'Quand la Cathédrale était blanche ce n'était pas des cénacles qui imposaient leur loi: Toute la ville était en marche'.[29] This sense of movement, maintained throughout the twelve-minute film by Franju's mobile camera, is also alluded to in a metaphor near the start of the commentary that is in tune with a modernist epigraph since it presents the medieval cathedral *as* modern, a weighty but graceful ship sailing through time: 'On avait délibérément tourné le dos à l'antique et lancé l'immense vaisseau de pierre blanche à des hauteurs inconnues, le plus haut qu'on avait pu'.[30] Just before this line Franju has employed superimposition, in an interesting frame of the cathedral reflected in the window of a toyshop, as if to highlight its difference from but continuing presence within a modern commercial world. *Notre Dame, cathédrale de Paris* ends as it began, in movement, as the camera descends from the heights of the cathedral exterior to the Place du Parvis Notre Dame, and opens up the shot horizontally to a barge moving along the Seine beyond the Ile St-Louis.

Unlike most of his later shorts, *Le Sang des bêtes* was Franju's personal project, not a commission or a request of any outside body, and he was obliged to obtain permissions to film in the abattoirs of la Villette and Vaugirard from the appropriate civic authorities: the Préfecture de la Seine for the outside of the abattoir buildings, and the

28 'Notre Dame's lookouts'.

29 'When the cathedral was white, it wasn't the cenacles who enforced their law: the whole city was on the move'.

30 'The cathedral's builders had deliberately turned their backs on ancient history and launched the immense vessel of white stone to unknown heights, as high as they could'.

Préfecture de la Police for the inside. In fact he went ahead with shooting after receiving a letter that granted him permission only to take photographs of the abattoirs' exteriors, and with no permission at all to photograph or film the interiors of the two sets of premises. He was excused when his lack of authorisation was discovered, however, since he was judged to have committed no impropriety (Brumagne 1977: 20–1).

The historical, memorising dimension of *Le Sang des bêtes* lies in the sections of the film that situate the La Villette and Vaugirard abattoirs in their Parisian locales – a kind of prologue, two intervals between the first and second and third and fourth sequences of slaughter respectively, and a short epilogue. These sections of the film are narrated by a female voice – the young woman seen embracing a man in the prologue – whereas a male voice narrates the 'abattoir' sequences of the film. Most of the unusual juxtapositions of images I shall discuss in Chapter 3 occur in the prologue – 'singuliers débris de vagues richesses'[31] dumped on waste ground that are picked out one by one by the camera after the opening shots of a bric-à-brac market, a modern apartment block and bare trees. Old radios, a naked mannequin of a woman without arms, a gramophone horn, and a Renoir painting sheltered by an open umbrella are some of these assorted objects, whose presence on the waste ground near the Porte de Vanves exposes the domestic life of the Parisians of this 'quartier' on the fringes of the administrative city. A passing train and a convoy of lorries on the boulevard nearby offset any quaintness suggested by Franju's photography of these objects. The prologue comes to a close with a shot of a commemorative bust of Emile Decroix, 'propagateur de la viande de cheval 1821–1900',[32] giving an idea of how long abattoirs have existed at the Vaugirard site. An interval between the first and second episode of slaughter in the central part of the film develops this historicising vein by filming the portrait photograph of Auguste Macquart, founder of the slaughterhouse 'à la fin du siècle dernier'.[33] The photograph of Macquart, grandfather of one of the 1948 abattoir's most skilled workers, depicts him proudly seated on a stool next to his freshly slaughtered horse lying in a pool of blood, and seems to be recalling a time even less sensitive to animals' fortunes

31 'the bizarre debris of uncertain riches'.
32 'horse meat merchant 1821–1900'.
33 'at the end of the last century'.

than the one *Le Sang des bêtes* mainly depicts. Interestingly, to close this episode Franju employs the cinematographic device of a theatre-style door closing, self-consciously drawing attention to his representation of the past in a device anticipating those to be used in *Hôtel des Invalides*. Before the second slaughter sequence come Franju's acclaimed shots of the Ourcq canal, and of the dark and sinister-looking factory architecture that surrounds it. In the much briefer interval between the third and fourth slaughter sequences a black bell tower is filmed against the sky, and identified as belonging to the site's auction house and not, as the commentary ironically states, to 'la gloire de saint Jean-Baptiste, patron des bouchers, ni à la mémoire de son agneau si doux'.[34] The image track in the epilogue to *Le Sang des bêtes* is a kind of summarised restatement of the location shots used in the prologue to the film and the two intervals described: throughout the film, there is a powerful sense of a locale at a very precise moment in time, still wholly in communication with its historic past, but on the verge of dramatic change.

Everyday and working life

After the scandal-tinged success of *Le Sang des bêtes*, secured in large part by a favourable review Jean Cocteau wrote for a Parisian daily (Brumagne 1977: 19),[35] Franju's was a name that circulated in the CNC and government departments with an interest in commissioning *courts métrages* from professional film-makers that could be distributed and shown as part of government's continuous efforts to motivate the French population in the reconstruction and modernisation of their country. Franju's next six films were all commissions produced with subsidies from the relevant government ministry.

As Franju's first 'film de commande', *En passant par la Lorraine* had disparate themes to organise – the historical, industrial and tourist-oriented aspects of the province it would present (Brumagne 1977: 24). Franju gave the film the title he did because the size of the province and its 500-year history meant that a short film could only

34 'the glory of St John the Baptist, patron saint of butchers, or to the memory of his gentle lamb'.

35 *L'Intransigeant*, 8 September 1949. Cocteau's review is reprinted in full in Maison de la Villette 1992: 31.

scratch the surface of the subject: his funding provided only for a four-day advance visit to Lorraine to plan the shooting (24). The two principal locations of the film are a village a few miles from Metz, and the mining district of Merlebach, identified as one of the most important mining districts in France. After an introductory section showing statues of Jeanne d'Arc in her native region, the province's capital Nancy, and architecture in Metz that secures the city its role as a symbolic centre of Lorraine's power and tradition, the action settles briefly in the village as it celebrates 14 July, Bastille Day and France's national holiday. Traditional costume, dancing and music-making are the order of the day, and the Mayor is seen inviting the prettiest girl in the village onto the dance floor. Amid the merry-making Franju inserts a striking freeze frame on a boy identified as the only survivor of the massacred population of Oradour-sur-Glane, a village on the other side of France but known to all through the horrific events of 1940. The entire film is thus structured by counterpoint: the sobriety of the longest section on Lorraine industry is offset by traditional but not strictly 'everyday' village celebrations, but the light-hearted tone of these scenes is in turn punctured by the shot of the boy-survivor, the reminder that the Second World War is only five years in the past, and that France's spiritual wounds have still to be healed, just as her economy and industry have to be rebuilt.

The longest, central section of *En passant par la Lorraine* closely follows the processes of the mining and steel industries – the transformation of coal into coke for use in blast furnaces, its transportation to factories in barges and along an elevated motorised conveyor belt, the smelting of metal and the production of sheet iron. A sense of the industries' power, precision and endlessly repetitive routines prevails through this part of the film. The most intense sequence, the filming of molten metal in its various forms, is unrelieved by the many groups of shots of industrial architecture and infrastructure that feature in the first and last part of the film's central section. Viewers recalling the surprising juxtapositions in the prologue of *Le Sang des bêtes* might have been struck by the disjunctures of atmosphere in shots of a blackened barge moving through idyllic, sunlit countryside, and of looming industrial chimneys behind a vast cornfield. Contrasts of black smoke with the white concrete of chimneys occur several times. In the many long shots of industrial landscapes interspersed with the 'factory interior' sequences, Franju uses wide angles and always shoots chimneys and cranes severally in order to give the frame a balanced or symmetrical set of contents. As the industrial section of the film comes to an end, the camera tracks away from the façade of some ruined factories to frame two enormous cooling towers, which are described as 'beautiful achievements' of industry. As Durgnat points out, however, the beauty Franju's film does find in industry is anything but the 'dismal liberalism' that results from glorification of the beauty of life-threatening industrial processes in Robert Flaherty's 1931 documentary *Industrial Britain* (Durgnat 1967: 43–4). The final minutes of *En passant par la Lorraine* return to diverse views of agricultural Lorraine, the link to which is made through a comparison of agricultural to industrial production. A château with a moat, churches, and the rooftops of villages and towns are shot against skies with magnificent cloud formations, the effects of light in these skies being far sharper in black and white than they would have been in colour, especially in contrast to the preceding dark industrial 'heart' of the documentary. A contrast in lighting also engineers the link to the film's close at the village's Bastille Day celebrations, as the camera picks up a torch in the darkness, part of the festivities' final procession.

A different type of industrial documentary from *En passant par la Lorraine*, *Les Poussières* devotes more of its content to scientific presentation of industrial and artisanal processes, and to the dangerous implications of regular or lifelong work in stone-crushing, porcelain-making and mining, the three industries Franju opts to depict. Since the film was commissioned by the Institut national de sécurité au travail, Franju was supposed to convey the advisability of wearing protective clothing at work. *Les Poussières* does indeed include sections on different types of protective masks and laboratory testing of their efficacy but, as Franju said later, he knew immediately he would have to extend the remit of the commission, because of the difficulty of recommending safety without first indicating what the dangers were. *Les Poussières* was to become the second instance in which Franju adapted a commission to suit himself while not mounting an explicit challenge to his sponsors.[36] The viewer was to be worried rather than reassured (Brumagne 1977: 32).

36 As Leblanc points out with respect to *Hôtel des Invalides*, Franju could 'ruiner le discours de l'institution militaire mais non ... substituer un autre discours explicite à ce discours. Le contexte de la commande interdit au cinéaste d'opposer une forme de propagande à une autre. Le cinéaste travaille dans l'implicite,

Franju's illustration of the pernicious effects of different types of industrial dust begins with the fine sand produced by the crushing of pebbles gathered from France's beaches, for use in cement making. (Such sand is rich in chemical elements harmful to humankind.) As in *En passant par la Lorraine*, the transport of raw material along conveyor belts, in trucks and in trains is shown; at this point, Franju introduces the issue of the risk of silicosis to workers. Harmful dust finds its way into water drained off from a rinsing facility into open country, after which the film moves to a Limoges porcelain factory, and covers in precise detail the stages involved in the manufacture of a single porcelain plate. Franju's commentary reveals that silica is one of the three main components of porcelain. A 'faiseur de bords',[37] who handles the assembled plates continuously in order to trim them to perfect proportions, is the most exposed worker in the factory, and is shown wearing no protective clothing whatsoever, without the commentary remarking on this further. The next scene lightens the grave atmosphere that is building up with shots of an acrobatic worker carrying a plank on which at least twenty plates are balanced. Another worker in constant contact with the porcelain and wearing no protective clothing is filmed, and an X-ray shot 'diagnoses' his silicosis of the lung.

The third industrial location of *Les Poussières* is a mountain colliery where scientists are investigating the dangers of mine dust to workers. Since the type of dust released by mining is already known to be 'la plus dangereuse de toutes'[38] (it is not specified whether this is particular to minerals in certain locations), they wear masks with filters. The quantities of dust released in controlled explosions to loosen rock are greater than in any other industry, some 200,000 million particles per litre of air, and this statistic introduces shots of various laboratory experiments to measure and analyse the dust's effects. Mine workers use a high-pressure jet to remove dust from

---

exerçant son activité critique à l'intérieur même du discours auquel il s'oppose' ('undermine the discourse of the military institution but not ... substitute another explicit discourse for it. The context of a commission forbids the film-maker from opposing one form of propaganda to another. The film-maker works in the implicit, exercising his critical activity inside the discourse he is opposing') (Leblanc 1992: 81).

37 'edge-maker'.

38 'the most dangerous of all'.

their grimy bodies, and a pipe exists to conduct away dust collected from the mine by aspiration, but the relative inefficacy of any attempts to combat the huge quantities of dust in the air is reinforced when we are told that the extraction of dust from the mine stops whenever there is a power cut. Trees have disappeared from the entire mountain valley where the mine is situated. A further scene of mask-testing in the laboratory is followed by a replay of shots of all the industrial facilities featured in the film, in order to emphasise that complete protection against the substances released by man's exploitation and engineering of the world's resources is simply not possible. To accompany *Les Poussières*' final image of a mushroom cloud rising from an atomic explosion, Franju asks an open but ironically intoned question, 'l'homme plus puissant que les éléments qu'il discipline sera-t-il préservé contre la mortelle radioactivité des poussières atomiques?'.[39]

Everyday and working life are equally to the fore in *Le Sang des bêtes*. The power with which Franju's best-known short portrays animal slaughter derives in part from its photography of butchery (knives, hands and corpses fill the frame in nearly all the shots taken inside the abattoirs), and partly from the highly structured manner in which these acts of slaughter are presented. Four sequences depict in turn the killing of one horse, a small number of cattle, a larger number of veal calves, and (finally) a large herd of sheep. By increasing the number of animals from sequence to sequence, Franju insists on the scale of the operation in which the abattoir workers are involved, its similarity to a factory floor. This ordering of sequences also progressively decreases the possibility of spectatorial identification with the animals' suffering, as the white horse that falls to its knees when shot between the eyes with a Behr pistol in the first sequence is a beautiful, noble animal, its head filmed in close-up as it is led in, whereas by the fourth and final sequence a detached and even humorous note creeps into the images of the waving feet of sheep's corpses. The slaughterers' work as trade is emphasised by an early shot of the different instruments employed to kill the animals, and to skin and prepare their corpses for auction. The danger of the abattoir workers' labour is signalled by the mention and shot of Ernest Breuyet, whose right leg had to be amputated after his femoral artery was severed

39 'will mankind, more powerful than the elements he dominates, be protected from the fatal radioactivity of atomic dust?'

during the 'fleurage' of a horse (the operation of removing its skin using a razor-sharp steel knife). Other workers are identified by their successes – Alfred Maquart one of the 'Meilleurs Ouvriers de France', Maurice Griselle former French boxing champion – and by their professional skills. But these introductions to individual workers are moments of respite in the atmosphere of slaughter that prevails in *Le Sang des bêtes*, conveyed by the steam rising from the streams of fresh blood that overflow the vessels held close to severed jugular veins, and for which channels are provided in the abattoir floors. The second slaughter sequence includes close-ups of one of these overflow channels of blood and of a worker smashing open the beast's skull in a succession of violent blows. At this point the commentary falls silent for the longest period in the film, as shots follow of the cutting of the cow's spinal chord and the severing of its feet, after which it is hoisted onto a winch to allow the extraction of its internal organs. The white, viscous stomach of the cow slides out onto the abattoir floor, where it is split and emptied of its black and presumably foul-smelling contents. In the third sequence, the slaughter of veal calves, Franju multiplies the number of close views of the physical labour of butchery in a rapid series of fixed shots of the workers' hands and the twitching of the dead animal's reflexes. The large number of animals involved in the fourth and last sequence further increases the sense of machine-like, routine labour comprised by abattoir work; one worker carries sheep to another to be decapitated swiftly and efficiently, after which they are lined up on a huge table, 'un minutieux travail à la chaîne'.[40] At this point, the progressive lightening of tone created through the four sequences of the film by increasingly emphasising the everydayness of slaughter allows a relaxation of intensity. All that figures is the prevailing good humour of the workers 'qui sifflent ou chantent en égorgeant',[41] Charles Trenet's 'La Mer' strikes up on the sound track, and the epilogue begins.

Le Théâtre national populaire, the fourth film in this group, follows Jean Vilar's TNP through rehearsals in Paris and Genevilliers, an industrial suburb of Paris and the only non-performing stop on its tour throughout France and other world cities. Despite the dominant presence of Vilar gently lecturing and coaxing his actors in rehearsals of Molière's *Don Juan* in Paris, and the tributes to two leading actors

40 'a meticulous assembly line'.
41 'whistling or singing as they butcher'.

of the age (Maria Casarès and Gérard Philippe) that follow later in the film, the emphasis here is on everyday routine and the ordinariness of backstage life. In Genevilliers, an actor is shown smoking a last-minute cigarette before his call, an unnamed actress shown reciting her lines and donning a wig, and another couple of actors (Daniel Sorano and George Wilson) singing and bickering in their small and undecorated dressing room. In a cinematographic device that identifies the TNP's tour rather than the company itself as the subject of the documentary, the curtain that seems to be opening on the scene starting in Genevilliers actually opens on to the rest of the film, the 'performance' that is the TNP's tour. No footage of the company abroad was actually shot: instead, Franju conveys the troupe's international travel by using an effect from silent and prewar film: a photograph album whose pages flip through pictures of London, Warsaw, Moscow, Athens and Venice. Marseilles, Bordeaux and Lyon are also mentioned in the commentary at this point, but the TNP's perform-ances are only actually filmed in Avignon, host to an annual theatre festival since 1947, where Casarès plays Lady Macbeth and Philippe the Prince of Denmark. The end of Lady Macbeth's 'out, out, damned spot' speech cuts to a brief excerpt of the conclusion of *Hamlet* and to the rapturous applause and curtain calls that follow.

Franju's final documentary to focus on the everyday lives and customs of the French in the 1950s is *Sur le pont d'Avignon*, his shortest film apart from the prewar *Le Métro* and shot as something of an afterthought to *Le Théâtre national populaire*, during the fortnight in July 1956 when Franju and his crew had to wait between the two Avignon theatrical performances that were to feature in the longer film (Cynthier Grenier, quoted in Vialle 1968: 172). There are three sections to *Sur le pont d'Avignon*: an introduction to Avignon's archi-tectural sights, an interlude showing the city's inhabitants at play, and coverage of the 14 July procession, dances, and fireworks. The film begins in mid-river, at the end of the famous old *pont d'Avignon* of the song, and a tracking shot along the river introduces the medieval papal palace (a masterpiece of gothic architecture) as the heart of the ancient city, with vertical tracking shots emphasising elevation just as they did in *Notre Dame, cathédrale de Paris*. Further architectural shots follow of the city's Grande Chapelle, of hunting frescoes from the work rooms of Pope Clemens VI, and of two scenes from the nearby ancient fortified city of Villeneuve-les-Avignon. After this historical and tourist-oriented introduction, the film's short second section focuses directly on the lives of the city's inhabitants, with shots of children flying kites, skipping and playing ball in the park. The link to the third section of the film is engineered through a self-conscious thematisation of movement and the image: the camera follows the children's ball as it bounces away from them down some steps and over to a kiosk at which a woman tourist is looking at (black and white) postcards of Avignon, including the *pont*, a *mise en abyme* of Avignon-as-tourist-destination that leads directly into images of the Bastille Day celebrations. The particular importance of these celebrations in Avignon is that 14 July, the national holiday of the Republic, symbolises freedom from papal authority; the irony behind Franju's film is that the 1956 processions and firework displays had actually been cancelled because of France's troubles over decolonisation, but were re-organised late in the day and staged in large part for his cameras. Shots of flags, of a military band, of women dancing in traditional costume, and of a procession moving through the city gradually pick up in pace to end in a whirl of fireworks and dancing: movement is constant as in so many of Franju's shots, and expresses the interplay between history and modernity found particularly in *Notre Dame, cathédrale de Paris*, while the film as a whole picks up the emphases on everydayness, traditional popular culture, and tourism found in several other of his *courts métrages*.

Movement, speed and modernity

The sense of movement that dominates *Notre Dame, cathédrale de Paris* and *Sur le pont d'Avignon* figures in most of Franju's other *courts métrages*, to differing degrees. *En passant par la Lorraine* begins in movement along a provincial road, and continues with a tracking shot across a darkened plain from the Verdun region to the city of Metz; the geographical shift between the two places is also the historical movement from the First World War to 1950. Amid the filming of the village Bastille Day celebrations a low-angle shot from beneath one of the horses on the merry-go-round communicates sensations of whirling and spinning. As the sequences of the film on industry begin, the camera tracks behind a coke truck through a manually operated gate to where the single line of track continues beyond, before going on to follow the industrial production line and the 'movement' (processing) involved in the transformation of matter from one state to another. In the final shots of the film the camera recedes into the darkness away from the torch-lit procession that is completing the village's Bastille Day celebrations, marking its departure from the Lorraine region.

Trains feature largely in *Les Poussières* as well as in Franju's two films about the Paris underground; in the introductory sequence on varieties of dust a train arriving in a smoky station illustrates the 'poussières des gares de Paris',[42] and industrial trucks on single lines of track figure even more prominently than in *En passant par la Lorraine*. More striking is an interfilmic reference to the Lumières' *Arrivée dans la gare de Ciotat*; the train rushes through Franju's frame at exactly the same angle as in the Lumières' film, with the telling difference that here it does not stop. A short episode in *Mon chien* features no fewer than four different modes of transport: the dog is awoken from his night in a field by a plane passing low overhead, and shortly afterwards encounters a busy road at a level crossing where a train is passing, motorbikes wait to cross from one direction, and a sports car from the other. The barge is another mode of transport that features significantly in *Les Poussières*, as it does in *Le Sang des bêtes* and *En passant par la Lorraine*. Contrast between a slower industrial age and the accelerated modernisation of 1950s France is suggested by the difference between the measured, stately progress of barges and the speed of trains and road transport. Evidence of the centrality of movement to Franju's cinematic vision is given by an indication included in instructions for a film he planned but never made, *Paris en bateau-mouche*, 'Ce film sera en continuel mouvement' (Vialle 1968: 114).[43] (The one *court métrage* of which Franju was not allowed the final cut, *Navigation marchande* (1954), is also an important reference here, for obvious reasons.)

The principal effect of a shot of lorries leaving the mountain colliery amid clouds of dust near the end of *Les Poussières* is to isolate and emphasise the central role played by transport – in this instance road transport – in contemporary industry. As I suggested above, the TNP's tour rather than the company itself is the main subject of *Le Théâtre national populaire*, and the part of the film devoted to the tour

42 'dust of Paris's stations'.

43 'This film will be continuously in movement'.

begins with a shot of a train steaming over a viaduct. More importantly, the film's final shot, accompanied by the modernist (melodious
but atonal) music of Maurice Jarre, is of the three lorries that transport the company's sets and equipment travelling along a provincial
road to its next destination. This image of a touring national company
indicates how fully mobile 1950s French society has become or is
becoming; as private car ownership increases dramatically, road
transport is also supporting the circulation of culture.

In all these instances mobility and speed are indicators of
modernity, signs of the rapid technological and cultural change
France was undergoing. Accompanying social change meant the
formation of new groups and classes in the population, and people
representing these classes also appear in Franju's *courts métrages*. The
opening location shots of the Palais de Chaillot in *Le Théâtre national
populaire* are followed by a shot of a young couple at the front of a
queue for tickets. A close shot of the same couple in the front row of
an audience follows the sequence of Jean Vilar rehearsing his actors,
accompanied by the commentary 'Les spectacles du TNP sont suivies
avec ferveur par le public de la banlieue parisienne':[44] the young
couple belongs to the new and rising social class of 'cadres'[45] that
developed in France in the late 1940s and 1950s. *Mon chien* features a
bourgeois family financially secure enough to live in a detached house
in the suburbs, own a car, and take holidays. The tourism *Mon chien*
alludes to, a significant element of the new consumer culture of the
1950s, is of course much more central to *En passant par la Lorraine*
and *Sur le pont d'Avignon*, films made in order to present and promote
a French province and city to prospective visitors. Tourism is also
implied yet subverted in Franju's critique of war in *Hôtel des Invalides*,
through the guided visit of the museum.

Paris and the Métro

Existing studies of Franju have little or nothing to say about Franju's
first film *Le Métro*, co-directed with Henri Langlois in 1934, which is
perhaps understandable given the circumstances in which it was shot

44 'the TNP's performances are followed fervently by the inhabitants of Paris's
    suburbs'.
45 'executives'.

and the amateurish quality of the result: Langlois and Franju were using a borrowed camera and three reels of 16mm film paid for by Langlois' family (Langlois and Myrent 1986: 31), and the film they put together is silent and only eight minutes long. Manipulation of the camera is sometimes uncertain (Durgnat 1967: 32). But examination of the editing of *Le Métro* reveals a rhetoric quite distinct from the rest of Franju's *courts métrages*, an urgent rhythm dependent on insistent repetition, and this makes it relevant to my discussion of the representation of modernity in Franju's *courts métrages*.

Le Métro consists mainly of shots of moving trains, primarily on over-ground sections of the Métro. But five types of shot occur in addition to these: (1) views from inside a train cab that record little but the impression of speed, (2) a set of shots down onto the top of trains passing under a bridge (just a blur of light-coloured movement, the content of these shots is initially difficult to identify), (3) close-up views of carriage doors and the automatic 'portillons' onto Métro platforms closing, (4) shots of the lifts taking passengers to and from the platforms, (5) a set of shots of passengers descending or ascending one of the flights of steps leading from pavement level down into a Métro station. The first two types of shot are repeated several times almost without variation, while the third and fourth types undergo generic repetition – that is, the actual automatic doors and lifts filmed are different, but the meaning and atmosphere of the shot is the same. The shots of passengers ascending from or descending into a station combine the two types of repetition, since the viewpoint itself is almost unvarying, but the flows of differently attired passengers create a sense of variation, without significant change in atmosphere or meaning.

Since *Le Métro* has no commentary and the sets of repeated images do not add up to any kind of narrative, the insistently repetitive editing of the film (for which it seems Langlois may have been mainly responsible, since Franju stated much later 'Moi, je voulais un mont-age d'idées, et lui souhaitait un montage de rythme'[46] (Carbonnier and Collombat 1986: 8)) gives it its only structure, and a palpable urgency combined with a non-progressive sense of movement. A highly ambivalent response to modernity is suggested: metal bars, tiles and the oppressive lattice-patterned ironwork of lifts and railings

46 'I wanted editing by ideas, and he wanted editing by rhythm'.

feature constantly, picked out in numerous vertical and horizontal tracking shots. Some of the shots of lifts and of the stone steps contain streams of daylight, and billows of steam entirely fill the space behind a latticework iron grille at one point, creating a high-contrast and formally pleasing shot. The prevailing atmosphere of the film is confined and dark, however, and although Franju and Langlois' camera seems fascinated by the fragments of mechanical modernity it captures, it is difficult to affirm that it creates a laudatory and forward-looking picture of that modernity.

Twenty-four years later, *La Première Nuit* offers up a totally contrasting vision of the Métro. Ghostly and labyrinthine, it is explored one night by a boy from a privileged bourgeois background who gives the slip to the chauffeur driving him home from school in order to follow his classmates underground. He is not reunited with his peers, but gets on and off trains and discovers the Métro's routes, maps and vast, echoing stations, particularly the central station of Cité. After walking past rats scurrying in a tunnel and up a staircase past a 'Montée interdite' notice,[47] the boy sits down tiredly on an immobile escalator, where he falls asleep. The remainder of the film depicts the dream he has during his night underground, and since this introduces questions of desire and relations between the sexes, I shall discuss it in Chapter 4. The reading of *La Première Nuit* I want to make here concerns its blend of fiction and documentary, which points both back through Franju's career in short film and forward to the *longs métrages* he was about to begin directing.

In the 1930s Franju and Henri Langlois had planned to co-direct a short film called *Le Métro fantôme*, for which they were envisaging décors by Méliès and a 'scénario fantastique et poétique de Jacques Prévert et J.B. Brunius' (Brumagne 1977: 27).[48] Nothing in Franju's comments about the project indicates a story resembling *La Première Nuit* (which is based on an idea by Marianne Oswald, and scripted by Oswald and Remo Forlani), but there is an unmistakable connection between the atmosphere suggested by 'fantôme' and the eerie, poetic cinematography of Franju's last short. In *La Première Nuit* the fantastic atmospheres of Cocteau's films are never far away; a shot of a long illuminated station tunnel directly resembles *La Belle et la bête*

47 'No entry'.
48 'a fantastic and poetic screenplay by Jacques Prévert and J.B. Brunius'.

(1946), while a lone cyclist passing with a lamp on his cycle recalls the encounters with solitary figures in *Orphée* (1950), and the glittering sparks of soldering torches give a fairytale aura to an image of men working on the track in a tunnel. *Le Métro fantôme* was never made because Méliès, in 1937 a very elderly man probably not well enough to do the work anyway, found the idea too 'pompes funèbres' (28).[49] Nonetheless, the existence of the project shortly after the making of *Le Métro* indicates the range and ambivalence of Franju and Langlois's vision of the Paris Métro, an ambivalence fully confirmed by *La Première Nuit*, where an unmistakably documentary interest in the Métro's architecture and the movement of its trains is inextricably melded to a storyline about adolescent desire and subterranean mystery. The photographer who realised Franju's ghostly vision in *La Première Nuit* was Eugen Shuftan, the experienced contributor to German expressionism who would create the atmospheres of *La Tête contre les murs* and *Les Yeux sans visage*. Franju's association with *cinéma fantastique* had already begun – or was beginning, just as his first opportunity to direct a full-length fiction film was about to arise. The experimentation with fiction in *La Première Nuit* is much bolder than in *A propos d'une rivière* and *Mon chien*, and Franju's last short is of particular significance to his career, both in aesthetic terms, and as a transition to his career as a director of feature films. Having considered it as such, I can now move on to Franju's *longs métrages*.

49 'funereal'.

References

Anon (1957) '6 personnages en quête d'auteurS', *Cahiers du cinéma* 71 (May), 16–29.

Brumagne, Marie-Madeleine (1977), *Georges Franju. Impressions et aveux*, Lausanne, l'Age d'Homme.

Buache, Freddy (1955) 'Les premiers films de Georges Franju', *Positif* 13 (March–April), 33–5.

Buache, Freddy (1957) 'Entretien avec Georges Franju', *Positif* 25–6 (autumn 1957), 13–21.

Carbonnier, Alain and Collombat, Boris (1986), 'Franju ou le fantastique au quotidien', *Cinéma* 369 (24–30 September), 8.

Demeure, Jacques and Kyrou, Ado (1956) 'Le plus grand cinéaste français', *Positif* 16 (May), 37–40.

Dorsday, Michel (1952) 'Le cinéma est mort', *Cahiers du cinéma* 16 (October), 55–8.

Durgnat, Raymond (1967), *Franju*, London, Studio Vista.

Fieschi, Jean-André and Labarthe, André S. (1963) 'Nouvel entretien avec Georges Franju', *Cahiers du cinéma* 149 (November), 1–17.

Forbes, Jill (1992), *The Cinema in France After the New Wave*, London, BFI/ Macmillan.

Gauthier, Guy (1995), *Le Documentaire, un autre cinéma*, Paris, Editions Nathan.

Jeancolas, Jean-Pierre (2000), 'The reconstruction of French cinema', in Elizabeth Ezra and Sue Harris (eds), *France in Focus*, Oxford, Berg, pp. 13–21.

Langlois, G.P. and Myrent, G. (1986), *Henri Langlois*, Paris, Editions Denöel.

Leblanc, Gérard (1992), *Une esthétique de la déstabilisation*, Paris, Maison de la Villette.

Maison de la Villette (1992), *Georges Franju cinéaste*, Paris, Maison de la Villette.

Odin, Roger (sous la direction de) (1998), *L'Age d'Or du Documentaire. Tome 1. Europe: Anneés cinquante*, Paris, L'Harmattan.

Porcile, François (1965), *Défense du court métrage français*, Paris, Les Editions du Cerf.

Ross, Kristin (1995), *Fast Cars, Clean Bodies: Decolonization and the Reordering of French Culture*, Cambridge MA and London, MIT Press.

Truffaut, François (1954) 'Une certaine tendance du cinéma français', *Cahiers du cinéma* 31 (January), 15–29.

Vialle, Gabriel (1968), *Georges Franju*, Paris, Seghers.

Vigo, Luce and Breton, Emile (dossier établi par) (1994), 'Le Groupe des trente, un âge d'or du court métrage?', *Bref* (Le magazine du court métrage) 20 (spring), 23–42. Contains articles by Jacques Floud, Jean-Pierre Jeancolas and interviews conducted by Luce Vigo.

2

Beyond *cinéma fantastique*:
genre in Franju's *longs métrages*

Anyone familiar with Franju's eight feature films would be likely to agree that he is not a director of 'genre' films of the type familiar from classic and contemporary Hollywood.[1] In this chapter, however, I want to argue that genre is central to his *longs métrages*, and that his relationship to genre film-making is just as strong as that of his contemporaries Jean-Luc Godard and Claude Chabrol, whose reputations in the 1960s were built partly on the successful incorporation of elements of *film noir* and the suspense thriller into their early work. To do this I shall rely on the idea of genre as a 'mark' made influential in contemporary genre theory by Jacques Derrida's essay 'The law of genre' (1980). In his essay, Derrida points out that in order to belong to a particular genre, texts have to be marked as so belonging by a designation which is itself not part of the text (or film), a label that introduces questions of inside, outside and borders into genre theory, and that can be shown to deconstruct the very notion of coherent, self-identical genres. Applying this idea to film studies, Peter Brunette and David Wills take the example of the western, and suggest that although six-guns, cowboys and a western locale may be marks of the genre 'western', '[they] will, unlike the texts in which they appear, themselves never belong to the genre of the Western ... A specific text containing these marks of genre will never simply belong to a genre because these marks refer to a system of difference outside any given genre' (Brunette and Wills 1989: 48). To summarise their argument about film genres,

1 Franju made eight feature films that were given a cinema release. He also made three feature-length films for television which I am not including in this study: *La Ligne d'Ombre*, *La Discorde* and *Le Dernier Mélodrame*.

Brunette and Wills quote Derrida himself: 'Every text *participates* in one or several genres, there is no genreless text; there is always a genre and genres, yet such participation never amounts to belonging' (48).

   Les Yeux sans visage and *Judex* remain Franju's best-known films, internationally as well as in France, and this is almost certainly because of their strongly marked relationship to *cinéma fantastique*. The critical and commercial reception of Franju's work has always been dominated by the *fantastique*, which has branded him as an *auteur* to such a degree that it has overshadowed the success he enjoyed as a director of documentaries in the 1950s. In the next chapter I shall seek to modify this interpretation of Franju's career by arguing that it is in his relationship to the 'real', established during his years in *court métrage*, that the wellspring of his film-making can be located, and that his feature films mark a continuation and development of this 'aesthetic realism' (Franju's own words and a problematic expression), not a relinquishing of it. In this chapter, then, I am suggesting, as I did at the end of Chapter 1, that there is continuity rather than any break between the singular vision of Franju's documentaries and the *fantastique* aesthetics, atmospheres and narratives to be found throughout his *longs métrages*.

Fantastique Franju?

Franju has not only consistently been received as a director of *cinéma fantastique*, he has represented France in international surveys of the genre. In a glossary of its fifty top directors included in a 1995 special issue of the journal *CinémAction*, Franju is the only French director listed apart from Jacques Tourneur, whose major films were all made after his emigration to Hollywood, in Val Lewton's unit at RKO studios in the 1940s. (Interestingly, Jean Cocteau is not included, although *La Belle et la bête*, *Orphée* and *Le Testament d'Orphée* earn Cocteau a place in most dictionaries of the *fantastique*.) The *CinémAction* entry illustrates very well how Franju's reputation as a director of the *fantastique* rests mainly on two films, *Les Yeux sans visage* and *Judex*, which are described as 'deux joyaux [qui] scintillent au panthéon du genre, au sein d'un cinéma français peu enclin à le manier'.[2] While it is important

---

2 'two jewels that sparkle in the pantheon of the genre, amid a French cinema rarely inclined to deal in it', Piton 1995: 167.

not to underestimate the role played by elements of the *fantastique* in Franju's cinema, since they are vital to *Les Yeux sans visage*, to *Judex* and to *Nuits rouges*, I shall argue against seeing any of these films as a pure example of the genre, and against the straightforward, essentialist understanding of Franju as a director of the *fantastique*, for two main reasons. The first is that since the era of classic film-making, usually understood to finish around 1960, the genre itself has gradually become so extensive as to be unwieldy, an over-inflated term that is of little help in critical discussion. (In terms of an Anglo-American approach to film genres *cinéma fantastique* includes science fiction, horror, pure fantasy and the fairy tale, 'but not the musical' (Austin 2001: 167).) My second reason for eschewing the *fantastique* as a genre label is simply that it does not adequately describe most of Franju's *oeuvre*, in which (as I shall go on to show) there are strong elements of *film noir*, of the thriller, and of melodrama, and which includes three full-scale literary adaptations. In a convenient critical act of legitimation, Franju has time and again been named to demonstrate that France does 'do' *cinéma fantastique*, since France otherwise has very little to contribute to the area. But although this labelling has a solid foundation in his *oeuvre*, the image of his cinema it has given rise to is inadequate. The adjustment to Franju's critical fortunes I am attempting in this chapter will be based largely on the argument that although the *fantastique* is an essential notion in appreciating and understanding his cinema, it should not be used *as a genre category* to classify, necessarily reductively, his *longs métrages*, either individually or as a set of eight films.

Starting with the three of Franju's films most often taken to represent the *fantastique* – *Les Yeux sans visage* (1959), *Judex* (1963) and his last cinema film *Nuits rouges* (1974) – I shall go on to look at the generic puzzle posed by his third, critically and commercially unsuccessful feature *Pleins feux sur l'assassin* (1961). I shall then consider two other genres strongly represented in Franju's feature films: *film noir* and melodrama. A separate part of the chapter will be devoted to the issue of literary adaptation. No fewer than five of Franju's feature films have their origins in novels, but his first two features *La Tête contre les murs* and *Les Yeux sans visage* use the novels from which they are drawn as source material, and are not literary adaptations as such – they are 'inspired by' rather than adaptations of Hervé Bazin's *La Tête contre les murs* and Jean Redon's *Celle qui n'était plus* respectively. The section of this chapter on adaptation – a genre category in its own right, despite the fact that adapted films are usually marked for another genre or genres as well – will look at the three of Franju's films planned and approached as full-scale adaptations: *Thérèse Desqueyroux*, *Thomas l'Imposteur*, and *La Faute de l'Abbé Mouret*.

Translating the *fantastique*: *Les Yeux sans visage*

Cinéma fantastique is a genre category specific to the critical traditions of France and some other European nations, such as Italy. It emerged early in the twentieth century out of the literary genre of the *fantastique*, to which many important Romantic and nineteenth-century French writers (Baudelaire, Maupassant, Zola) had contributed. The main counterparts of *cinéma fantastique* in other national and transnational traditions are horror and science fiction; 'horreur' or the 'film d'épouvante' is a large subset of what French film writing terms the *fantastique*, and postmodern and contemporary horror films such as Wes Craven's *Scream* trilogy and the Spanish director's Alejandro Almenàbar's *Los Otros/The Others* continue to be written up in French journals aimed at avid followers of this kind of cinema, such as *L'Ecran fantastique*. Following the international pre-eminence in horror production by Hollywood's Universal studios in the 1930s, the 1950s boom in American science-fiction 'monster' movies and the spectacular success of Britain's Hammer studio took horror cinema into its modern age. In the 1950s and 1960s, however, French film journals declined to view horror as a separate genre by continuing to locate it within the category of the *fantastique*. As critical writing on horror started to develop, a strong difference emerged between the anglophone and continental European reception of the genre. As Pam Cook summarises in *The Cinema Book*,

> Historical approaches [to horror] demonstrate a heterogeneity of inputs and developments rather than the integrated evolution of generic tradition attributed to the western or gangster film – e.g. Universal's gothic horror films of the 30s; German Expressionism; 50s science fiction monster movies; Hammer horror in the UK; Corman's Poe cycle; the onset of the psychological thriller with *Psycho* ... A tension remains between older European traditions and Hollywood, producing

the problem of relating the forms which developed in the European art cinema in terms of the 'fantastique' or supernatural and the formation of a popular Hollywood genre. (Cook 1985: 99)

These are the terms in which I want to consider *Les Yeux sans visage*, which can be considered 'classic' horror because it was made before the 1960 watershed that Hitchcock's *Psycho* has come to represent for criticism of the genre.[3] Although it has seldom (if ever) been considered in its historical context, *Les Yeux sans visage* in fact makes an extremely interesting case study of the multiple cross-currents in international horror production in the 1950s: it is linked to German expressionism and early European horror through the aesthetic created by photographer Eugen Shuftan, has narrative affinities with the Universal horror films of the 1930s (especially *The Bride of Frankenstein*), and coincides historically and in narrative terms with 1950s science-fiction monster movies.

Even before *Les Yeux sans visage* was released in Paris on 2 March 1960, expectations were running high, in part because several spectators had fainted at a non-commercial screening organised by the 'Fédération française des ciné-clubs' (Alain Saunders, *L'Express*, 23 July 1959). Gore, an aspect of horror cinema that would only come into its own in the 1960s and 1970s, figures prominently in *Les Yeux sans visage* for a film of its time, and audiences reacted accordingly, most famously at the showing that opened the 1960 Edinburgh festival, during which no fewer than seven spectators had to be carried from the auditorium (Fieschi and Labarthe 1963: 15). Unsurprisingly in the wake of this event, the British press responded to the film with barely disguised disgust (Durgnat 1967: 79), but despite a rejection from Britain and a few French critics of the aesthetic territory it was exploring, Franju's film was widely distributed across Europe. The release of a dubbed American version entitled *The Horror Chamber of Dr Faustus* then helped the film gain the cult following among horror fans and cinephiles it has retained ever since, a following which explains why it is the only film of Franju's to have remained commercially available on video and to have been transferred to DVD.[4] *Les*

3 For example, in Paul Wells' recent useful *The Horror Genre* (2000). *Les Yeux sans visage* is omitted altogether from Wells' book, I would suggest, because of the difficulties it poses to a classificatory history of the genre.

4 Durgnat quotes Pauline Kael's description of the 'urban American response' to the film at length (Durgnat 1967: 84).

Yeux sans visage was given a second major cinema release in France in September 1986, timed to coincide with a retrospective of all Franju's films organised by the French Cinémathèque for its own fiftieth anniversary (Forestier 1986). French reviewers' responses from 1986 are unanimously positive, far more uniformly so than those of 1960, and reflect the status of genre classic *Les Yeux sans visage* had by then acquired.

On the occasion of its 1986 re-release, a lengthy review of *Les Yeux sans visage* and of Franju's contribution to French cinema was penned by Serge Daney, film critic of *Libération* and former editor-in-chief of *Cahiers du cinéma* (Daney 1986). Tellingly, the first issue Daney raises, in the subtitle of his article, is genre, by saying that *if* a 'grand cinéma français fantastique' had existed, *Les Yeux sans visage* is what it would have looked like. In other words, Daney regrets the lack of a real tradition of the *fantastique* in France, but suggests that *Les Yeux sans visage* is a great enough film ('Une merveille' [A marvel]) to compensate for this lack, at least to some degree. Since he has the benefit of hindsight, Daney's reflections contextualise *Les Yeux sans visage* within French national cinema, but as I have already noted, responses to the film in 1960 were considerably more surprised by Franju's move into genre film-making, and less convinced by the results. Two main types of criticism were made, the first of which was a complaint that the gory aesthetics and fear-inducing plot of *Les Yeux sans visage* were no more than a tired repetition of the classics of German expressionism, or perhaps a belated homage to Fritz Lang (*La Croix* 17 March 1960; *France-Observateur* 10 March 1960). The second type of criticism was snobbishness about Franju's 'descent' from auteurist *court métrage* into a genre that many saw as minor and unimportant, a reaction undoubtedly fuelled by the fact that the source novel of *Les Yeux sans visage* had appeared in a collection parallel to Gallimard's 'Série noire', the 'Angoisse' collection of the Editions Fleuve Noir. One reviewer sneered at the 'odéonisme' of Franju's film (*France-Observateur* 10 March 1960), one called its subject and screenplay 'puérile' (*Noir et blanc* 11 March 1960), while another said *Les Yeux sans visage* was to *Le Sang des bêtes* and *Hôtel des Invalides* as the Musée Grevin (Paris's waxwork museum) was to the Louvre (*Les Arts* 16 March 1960). In the eyes of these critics, Franju was throwing his proven talent as a director away, not because he had made a bad film, but because horror cinema was 'un genre mineur assez indigne de ses possibilités' (*Juvénal* 16 March 1960).[5] In one interview Franju responded to these criticisms by saying that the infusion of fear and the horrible into realist narrative he had achieved in *Les Yeux sans visage* was a deliberate attempt to get a minor genre taken seriously (*L'Humanité* 2 March 1960): it seems more likely that *Les Yeux sans visage*'s mixture of poetic aesthetics and pulp narrative was determined more by other, unplanned factors, but Franju's defence of his film's place in the burgeoning popular culture of the time does at least indicate that he did not share the snobbishness of his critics.

Les Yeux sans visage's unusual infusion of pulp narrative into beautiful, velvety photography, which was to be continued in two of Franju's next three features (*Pleins feux sur l'assassin* and *Judex*), was largely due to the partnership between the film's director and the adapters of Jean Redon's novel for the screen, Pierre Boileau and Thomas Narcejac, key names in the history of literary and cinematic detective fiction (Bellour and Lacassin 1961). Although Redon, Franju himself and Claude Sautet also collaborated on the adaptation, the careful crafting and pacing of the film's narrative, and the changes it displays from the novel's 'family romance' (which I shall discuss in Chapter 4), must be attributed partly to the Boileau–Narcejac pairing, acclaimed for their work on Clouzot's *Les Diaboliques* (1954) and Hitchcock's *Vertigo* (1958). Boileau and Narcejac's work adds a further dimension to the genre(s) of *Les Yeux sans visage*, which thereby becomes not just a *film fantastique* and a horror film, but a 'polar' as well, anticipating the fuller exploration of the 'film policier' Franju would undertake in *Pleins feux sur l'assassin*. A significant part of the plot of *Les Yeux sans visage* deals with the police investigation into the disappearance of the young women Dr Genessier has had abducted for his operating theatre, and to begin with the police are represented as genial, ingenious and sympathetic. Ultimately, however, their investigation proves completely ineffectual, an element of the plot undoubtedly intended by Franju as a critique of the institution of the law, his dislike of which was as vehement as his distrust of the Church and of the army.

In these comments on *Les Yeux sans visage* I have tried, rather than giving a reading of the film (which has already been treated to countless appreciative critical readings) to describe it and its reception

5 'a minor genre quite unworthy of his abilities'.

in terms of cinematic genre, and to hold it up as a kind of example of Franju's relationship to genre cinema. This relationship is complex and above all plural: *Les Yeux sans visage* was received by most of its spectators and critics as a horror film,[6] and therefore also from the continental European point of view, as a *film fantastique* (the journal *L'Ecran fantastique* devoted substantial coverage to it on its release, and took it as a kind of paradigm for Franju's subsequent *longs métrages*, with the exception of his literary adaptations). Since 'policier' elements also feature in the film, *Les Yeux sans visage* can reasonably be asserted to be participating in at least three genres. Rather than try to limit this multiple participation by imposing on it the (admittedly expansive) generic identity of a *film fantastique*, I would like to embrace the plurality of the film's generic markers, and suggest that such a multiple identity and 'belonging' to plural genres is what characterises Franju's feature film-making as a whole. Film genres are composite constructions that can be subdivided in almost unlimited ways: a good example of this is the description of *Les Yeux sans visage* as 'gothic' cinema, an adjective that harks back to the origins of *littérature fantastique* from which the related film genre sprang. Franju's fullest exploration of the 'gothic' probably lies in the location and interiors in which he filmed *Pleins feux sur l'assassin*, and in my reading of that film I shall be opening up this further sub- or pre-category of *cinéma fantastique*. First, however, I shall continue my discussion of the *fantastique* by looking at *Judex*, and at *Nuits rouges*.

Glamour in *mode rétro*: Franju's homages to Louis Feuillade

Louis Feuillade's original, silent *Judex*, of which Franju's film may be considered a kind of remake, appeared in 1916. Coming in the wake of Feuillade's hugely successful popular thrillers *Fantômas* (1913) and *Les Vampires* (1915), adaptations from the pulp novels by Pierre Souvestre and Marcel Allain, it was released in cinemas in twelve weekly episodes and garnered an enormous following. Unlike *Fantômas* and *Les Vampires*, however, *Judex* was made for the cinema before being transferred to novel form, in response to wartime demand for a more

6 As Durgnat points out, *Les Yeux sans visage* anticipates *Psycho* in narrative form: 'a first heroine visits "Hell", is killed, and a second victim nearly takes her place' (Durgnat 1967: 82).

morally reassuring hero: the thoroughgoing evil of *Fantômas* had been the core of the protagonist's popularity, but in the middle of the Great War this thrilling crime and malevolence required some counter-balancing. In Feuillade's *Judex* the actions of the chief character are morally motivated, since his Corsican mother has compelled both Judex and his brother to swear to avenge their father, who committed suicide after being ruined by the corrupt banker Favraux. This revenge plot is entirely missing from Franju's film, which is in most respects a highly faithful recreation of Feuillade's story: both films begin with Favraux's receipt of threatening letters signed 'Judex' and apparent sudden death at a lavish masked ball organised to celebrate the engagement of his fragile and beautiful daughter Jacqueline. Judex and his followers have in reality kidnapped Favraux. A spate of break-ins, pursuits and kidnappings follow, in which Judex's mission is to rescue Jacqueline from the clutches of her father's hangers-on, principally the evil Diana Monti, known previously to Favraux and Jacqueline as Marie Verdier, the governess of Jacqueline's daughter Alice. In a final confrontation at an empty suburban house the involve-ment of the ineffectual detective Cocantin, hired by Favraux before his kidnapping, finally proves of some use when he is able to draw on the assistance of the acrobat Daisy and men from her circus troupe. Diana Monti and her lover–assistant Moralès are defeated when she falls to her death after a rooftop struggle with Daisy, Favraux commits suicide, and Judex and Jacqueline can finally be united.

As Durgnat points out, Judex 'is the original caped crusader' (Durgnat 1967: 107), beating Batman to the role by some years. But in Franju's film the moral motivation of the righter of wrongs 'justicier' Judex is almost entirely absent. According to Franju his scriptwriter – Jacques Champreux, Feuillade's grandson – and his dialoguist on the film, Francis Lacassin, were chiefly responsible for writing the revenge plot out of the original *Judex* story, but Franju's view of this was that 'motivations vengeresses'[7] had deprived Judex's character of mystery that he might now gain: 'L'histoire, maintenant "épurée" de sa morale, trouvera, nous l'espérons, son harmonie' (Fieschi and Labarthe 1963: 16).[8] As he also points out, Judex's protective and defensive quest to punish corruption and cruelty uses techniques hardly less villainous than those of his enemies; Judex is at least as much of a bastard as

7 'vengeful motivations'.
8 '"Purged" of its morality, the story will now, we hope, find its harmony'.

Favraux (17), a sadist who kidnaps, imprisons and tortures his foe (Beylie and Schapira 1984: 8). The most convincing explanation for the kind of reorientation of Feuillade's narrative Franju makes, therefore, is probably his longstanding desire to remake *Fantômas* rather than any of Feuillade's other films, a wish he mentions in interviews from the mid-1950s onwards, and which seemingly nearly came to fruition in 1961, only to be disappointed when the offer was made to André Hunebelle instead, the result being the commercially highly successful trio of films *Fantômas* (1964), *Fantômas se déchaîne* (1965), and *Fantômas contre Scotland Yard* (1966).[9] As a number of press reviews of *Judex* observed in 1963, another way in which Franju seems to have compensated for not being able to make *Fantômas*, whether consciously or unconsciously, is by tipping the dramatic interest of his film from Judex towards the villainous Diana Monti, played by Francine Bergé in an almost universally admired performance. Despite his commanding appearance in black cape and broad-brimmed hat – an authority reinforced by the actor hired for the role, the athletic and graceful American stage magician Channing Pollock – Judex is an undeniably ineffectual hero, who fails to look behind him, lets his foe escape, and in the end relies on reinforcements to defeat her. Diana Monti is a stronger agent than Judex of the film's narrative, and the focus of its dramatic interest.

The consequences of Franju and Champreux omitting the history of Judex's motives for his actions from their homage to Feuillade can be felt in the tone and atmosphere of *Judex 1963* (a first remake of the film had already been done by Champreux's father Maurice, Feuillade's chief operator and later assistant director, in 1933). The overall 'feel' of Franju's *Judex* is dreamy, lyrical and magical; psychological interest in its characters is entirely passed over in favour of unexplained and therefore mysterious twists and turns in the action. Examples of this are the apparent sudden death of Favraux at the masked ball before he so much as sips the drink that has just been put in his hand, and his equally unexplained ressucitation some days later in Judex's underground lair. The atmosphere of Franju's *bal masqué* is otherworldly, and enhanced by the magnificent bird-mask worn by

9 Franju, predictably, disliked Hunebelle's films, and Freddy Buache calls them 'un désastre ... sans l'ombre d'un rapport avec la fantaisie noire de Pierre Souvestre et Marcel Allain' ('a disaster ... without any hint of a relationship with Pierre Souvestre and Marcel Allain's black fantasy') (Buache 1996: 52).

Judex as he performs conjuring tricks to the guests. The silent appearance of huge Alsatian guard-dogs as Diana Monti and Moralès try to kidnap Jacqueline from the deserted château (unsuccessfully on this occasion) is redolent with mystery and wonder, as is the remarkable set piece in the film's final sequence, when Judex's four caped reinforcements scale the end-wall of a six- or seven-storey apartment block unaided by hooks or crampons. Francine Bergé's costumes afford many instances of captivatingly bizarre, poetic images: disguised as a nun from the order of St Vincent de Paul, Diana Monti stabs Jacqueline with a drug-filled syringe as she exits from a station she has been lured to by a false alarm concerning her daughter Alice, an image of a murdering nun that provides strangely contradictory pleasures. More infamous in the history of the film is Bergé's 'striptease' from her nun's habit down to her black catsuit when her only escape lies by diving down through a trap door and swimming away through the mill race. As one reviewer put it, the whole of *Judex* reminds us that film is a privileged medium for the expression of poetic magic ('Judex battu par les femmes', *France-Observateur* 30 January 1964). Other reviewers link magic to the 'insolite' and describe the entire film as charming and bewitching, 'un pur divertissement, un pur charme, une réussite totale' ('Souris d'hôtel, bottes noires et passages secrets...', *L'Express* 30 January 1964).[10]

As all these scenes and comments start to show, Franju's aim in remaking *Judex* was primarily to create an aesthetically enhanced version of Feuillade's world that could communicate magic, poetry and the *fantastique*. Period interiors were precisely reconstructed, and some typical effects from Feuillade and his age – the arabesque flourishes framing the intertitles, irising in and out, even one keyhole shot – carefully retained. Plasticity was more important in *Judex* than in any other of his films, Franju stated (Fieschi and Labarthe 1963: 15). His photographer Marcel Fradetal went to extraordinary lengths to recreate the qualities of Feuillade's orthochromatic film, by imitating Feuillade's photographer Guérin and by arranging lighting so that décor and the character(s) in shot could be lit at the same time, rather than one at the expense of another (Marlore and Beylie 1963). The costumes for the film were designed by Christine Courcelles, who used magazines from the 1912–18 period to get the styles exactly

10 'pure entertainment, pure charm, a total success'.

right ('La nouvelle mission de *Fantômas*', *Les Lettres françaises* 23 January 1964). What carried the film was 'le côté décoratif esthétique' ('Des aventures oniriques en images d'Epinal', *Arts* 27 November 1963).[11] Possibly as a consequence of Franju's concentration on style, plasticity and effect, however, his *Judex* has a perceptible lack of narrative drive remarked on by a number of reviewers at the time, who called its rhythm 'paresseux' and the directing 'nonchalante, pour ne pas dire laborieuse' (*Les Nouvelles littéraires*, 20 January 1964).[12] Impressive though its set pieces were, the film relied on them too much and seemed not to be able to link them up (*Le Monde*, 1 March 1964); its approach to the story's fantastic episodes and images was too studious, and lacked panache (*La Lanterne*, 9 April 1964). The actors had an absent air that seemed to result from not identifying with their roles, and the mystery and poetry of Franju's *mise-en-scène* faded as the film progressed because it had been created too obediently, 'avec une piété de conservateur de cinémathèque' (*Le Figaro*, 21 September 1964).[13] Perhaps the best summary of these weaknesses in narrative construction was given by Claude Mauriac in *Le Figaro littéraire*, who stated that the spectator of *Judex* was prevented from identifying with the action because the attention to single images and 'plastic beauty' demanded of him or her interfered too much with this process (*Le Figaro littéraire*, 30 January 1964). Critical reception of the film was generally very admiring of the homage to early cinema Franju had created – its 'retro' mode – but aware too of problems that had resulted from an over-conscientious approach to style and atmosphere.

Franju was a self-declared admirer of Feuillade, although he specified that it was Souvestre and Allain's books rather than the films that he had avidly consumed as an adolescent.[14] He did not actually see the twelve episodes of Feuillade's *Judex* until the opportunity to make his own film arose, upon which he and Jacques Champreux visited Brussels to watch it at the Belgian Cinémathèque. Franju's comment on the film later was that '*Judex* soit le seul film de Feuillade

11 'the decorative, aesthetic aspect'.
12 'lazy' and 'nonchalant, not to say laborious'.
13 'with the piety of a film archivist'.
14 'I didn't see Feuillade's *Fantômas* until I was about thirty, whereas I was brought up on Souvestre and Allain ... I read the Souvestre-Allain books when I was about fourteen' (Franju in Milne 1975: 69).

qui ne soit pas du bon Feuillade' (Carbonnier and Collombat 1986: 8);[15] he had certainly not seen anything like Feuillade's total output, but he clearly admired *Fantômas* much more than *Judex*, which he also said lacked humanity and drama (Fieschi and Labarthe 1963: 17). Although I do not disagree with Franju's own explanations of how *Judex*'s fantastic atmosphere and tone arise out of its representation of reality – a world whose moral dramas have been deprived of history in favour of their mythical appearances – I do want to question the classification of the film as a type of *cinéma fantastique* inherited or copied from Feuillade. *Judex* was unquestionably made in homage to Feuillade, but the result is stylistically and generically a very different proposition. In order to pursue this argument I turn now to the last of Franju's eight feature films, *Nuits rouges*, shot in 1973 and released in cinemas in 1974. Despite the ten-year interval between *Judex* and *Nuits rouges*, there are important links between the two films, as will soon become clear.

Nuits rouges is the title of the 100-minute cinema release of a production commissioned for French television and shown in eight separately entitled TV episodes under the overall title of *L'Homme sans visage*. As the film's modest number of reviewers noted at the time, it is impossible to miss the close resemblance of its villainous protagonist to Feuillade's Fantômas, who appears similarly masked and entirely black-clad in several episodes of the original five-and-a-half hour serial.[16] Freddy Buache's interpretation of Franju's project – that it was a homage to *Fantômas* the director had only been able to achieve in *Judex* 'au niveau de la plastique'[17] because Judex, an 'héros blanc', did not fundamentally suit him nearly as well as the 'héros noir' Fantômas (Buache 1996: 60) – is irresistible. *Nuits rouges/ L'Homme sans visage* draws on the age-old legend of the Order of the Knights Templar to construct an adventure that seems bizarrely adrift in history, revolving as it does around lost treasure, murder, underground ceremonies, crazed scientists (a genre-perfect performance by Clément Harari as Docteur Dubreuil), and radio-controlled taxis driven by robots. Location of the treasure of the Knights Templar is a

15 '*Judex* is the only film of Feuillade's that isn't good Feuillade'.
16 Feuillade in fact even directed a film entitled *L'Homme sans visage* in 1919, whose villain was presumably a Fantômas derivative, but there is no evidence to suggest that Franju had seen it or was aware of its existence.
17 'in terms of plasticity of form'.

secret Maxime de Borrego may have taken to his grave when murdered by the man-without-a-face for failing to surrender the information, and a race to recover it takes place between Borrego's nephew Paul and his girlfriend Maxine, assisted by the English historian Professor Petri, and the man-without-a-face and his glamorous Musidora-lookalike accomplice, backed up by Docteur Dubreuil and the zombie army he is building by surgically de-activating human brains. The Knights Templar defeat the forces of the man-without-a-face, and the treasure remains in their hands.

Nuits rouges was made on a budget so modest that Franju was obliged to shoot all its interiors in the studio (Milne 1975: 70), and this and Eastman colour give it an aesthetic that is claustrophobic, and more televisual than cinematic. As one reviewer pointed out, this has the appropriate effect of emphasising that the heirs to and 1970s equivalents of *Fantômas* in the entertainment world were serial spectaculars like the Bond films and television series such as 'The Man from U.N.C.L.E.' (Thirard 1975: 60). The role of the man-without-a-face is played by Jacques Champreux, Franju's scriptwriter on the film as on *Judex*, who also appears in an assortment of disguises in other cameo roles, most notably in drag as Mme Ermance, whose curio shop 'Au bonheur des dames' serves as a cover for the man-without-a-face's operations. The final scene of the film, in which a smart lime-suited Gayle Hunnicutt (the glamorous accomplice) is seen leaving the neighbourhood of the shop with her aged 'aunt' Mme Ermance on her arm, is very suitably 'feuilletonesque'; the story of this arch-criminal's quest for mastery could easily pick up directly from this point. In other respects, however, the abbreviation of a much longer TV serial into a feature-length cinema release leads to unevennesses in the drama, a problem of which Franju was aware (Schlockoff 1979: 68). But he enters into the film's world of pulp drama with less control and far more glee than in *Judex* ('Franju s'amuse comme un gamin. Nous aussi'[18] (Buache 1996: 60)), with the result that the film was much appreciated by some reviewers.[19] As one of them put it, it is a film 'qui demande qu'on joue le jeu qu'il

---

18 'Franju amuses himself like a child, and so do we'.
19 Viviani 1974; Thirard 1975. Having championed Franju in the 1950s, *Positif* failed to review any of his feature films after *Judex* except *Nuits rouges*, which *Cahiers du cinéma* did not cover.

nous propose'[20] (Thirard 1975: 53) – a light-hearted excursion into the 'merveilleux' that contains some glossy and dreamlike photography. Its daytime scenes in Paris and London are flat and oddly lacking in drama, but these alternate with 'des envolées oniriques où le réel perd son poids'[21] (53), of which the best instance is a moonlit sequence of Gayle Hunnicutt stealthily moving across rooftops, sliding down through skylights, and blowing poisoned darts at her targets. All the tried-and-tested devices of the *feuilleton* are marshalled to enjoyable effect.

It is hard to decide, though, to what degree *Nuits rouges* is an appreciative neutral pastiche of Feuilladian *réalisme fantastique* and to what degree, if any, it is a parody. Franju makes no attempt to periodise the narrative as he did with *Judex*, and as a result it sits uncomfortably in a contemporary metropolitan environment. It suffers from some of the same languours as *Judex*, soundly constructed as a narrative but often slowed down by the painstakingly arranged photography and set pieces of action – the ceremony to anoint a new Grand Master of the Order of the Knights Templar is an example – that do not procure as much visual pleasure as they seem intended to. The second of *Positif*'s reviews of the film affirms that Franju and Champreux must have thought about eliciting a 'second-order', reflexive response to the film's homage to the serial and then rejected the option – but that such a response is nonetheless possible (Thirard 1975: 60). This admiration of the way *Nuits rouges* shifts between different levels of imitation seems to me over-generous to the film, whose playfulness with cultural references creates as much confusion as entertainment; the best examples of this are the zombie army and the waxwork 'driver' of the remote-controlled taxi, which belong to science fiction, but connote a futurism already outdated by the early 1970s. According to Freddy Buache, the film begins in 'serious' homage to popular expressionism (dramatic lighting, colour symbolism, a gamut of exaggerated performances and costumes) but is quickly overtaken by sarcasm and parody (Buache 1996: 60–1). What is certain is that *Nuits rouges* was conceived in relation to Feuillade's serials at a moment when such nostalgia-driven cinema was not at all in vogue, and when the character of Fantômas had been supplanted by more modern and postmodern heroes, many of them conceived for the medium of television. The mixed and often mocking critical reception

20 'which asks us to play its game'.
21 'oneiric flights of fancy in which reality loses its weight'.

accorded to the film is shot through with an awareness that Franju had made only two feature films since 1965, and that his *Nuits rouges/ L'Homme sans visage* was a self-indulgence to compensate for the *Fantômas* producers had never chosen him to make, rather than entertainment calculated to please audiences.

Gothic 'polar' or 'exercice de style'? *Pleins feux sur l'assassin*[22]

Pleins feux sur l'assassin, Franju's eagerly awaited follow-up to *Les Yeux sans visage*, was shot during 1960 and released in Paris on 31 March 1961. Responses from the press during April 1961 were varied, but dominated by a sense of disappointment for which reviewers proffered different explanations: Franju had been let down by his material (the plot of *Pleins feux sur l'assassin* was too slight), did not have a clear idea of where he was going with *long métrage* directing, or – more interesting for my purposes in this chapter – had attempted too complex and too precise a mix of generic features, which had failed to cohere and which somewhat confused his audiences. The reviewers of *Les Arts* and *France-Observateur* took Franju to task for shamelessly 'borrowing' his plot from Agatha Christie's novel *Ten Little Niggers* (*Les Arts* 12 April 1961); *Le Canard enchaîné* lambasted *Pleins feux* as simply 'un film raté'[23] (*Le Canard enchaîné* 5 April 1961), and other reviewers termed it 'un pétard mouillé'[24] (*Paris-presse* 5 April 1961) and a futile cause (*Les Nouvelles littéraires* 21 April 1961). Since the Boileau-Narcejac 'double act' had been central to the appeal and the success of *Les Yeux sans visage*, a 'triple refinement' had been expected of the renewed collaboration between them and Franju (*Télérama* 16 April 1961), but Boileau-Narcejac's original screenplay was in fact singled out for its weakness by *Le Canard enchaîné* and *La Voix du Nord* (14 April 1961). One feature of *Pleins feux* that did meet with consistently appreciative and admiring remarks was its photography, with which both Franju and Marcel Fradetal were credited (*Le Figaro*

---

22 The actual expression 'polar gothique' is used of the film by Bernard Queysanne (Maison de la Villette 1992: 128). *Les Yeux sans visage* was also described as 'Gothic cinema', by Michel Delahaye in the title of his review for *Cahiers du cinéma* 106, 'Gothique flamboyant'.

23 'a failure'.

24 'a damp squib'.

9 April 1961; *Télérama* 16 April 1961). From what they knew of the plot, the cast and the locations, critics were anticipating 'un film de suspense et d'humour'[25] (*Combat* 5 January 1961) that continued to exploit and develop the *fantastique* décors and atmospheres from which Franju's name had become inseparable, but although many of them found mystery, suspense and some good gags, they were evidently disappointed by the film as a whole – the lack of impact and coherence being the fundamental problems detected by many of their reviews and articles. *Pleins feux sur l'assassin* simply seemed (and still seems, when compared to *La Tête contre les murs*, *Les Yeux sans visage* and all Franju's later features except probably *Nuits rouges*, whose weaknesses and poor critical fortunes I have already discussed) far more lightweight than audiences and critics had come to expect of the director of *Le Sang des bêtes*, *Hôtel des Invalides* and his first two substantial *longs métrages*. Despite visually resplendent locations, and fine performances from Jean-Louis Trintignant, Pierre Brasseur and a number of others, a typical neutral reviewer's summary of it was 'un innocent petit film, divertissement modeste et sans grand intérêt' (Pierre Marcabru, *Combat* 4 April 1961).[26] The high hopes placed in Franju as a director of *longs métrages* at the end of the 1950s undoubtedly suffered a setback from his third feature when it appeared at the very start of the new decade.

The plot of *Pleins feux sur l'assassin* certainly classifies it as a 'film policier', or 'polar' as the French thriller/crime drama had come to be known by the 1960s. (The 1950s had been a particularly successful decade for the 'polar', represented in France chiefly by the films of Jean-Pierre Melville and certain other classics such as Jacques Becker's *Touchez pas au grisbi*.) In a kind of prologue to the film, the aged patriarch of a Breton chateau, the Comte Hervé de Kéraudren (a very brief appearance by Pierre Brasseur) retires into a 'cachette'[27] located behind a drawing-room mirror to die. When summoned a day or two later by the Count's lawyer, the seven nephews and nieces who are heirs to the castle are told that quirky article 115 of the civil code states that they will not be able to lay claim to their inheritance for five years, because their uncle's body has not been found ('Médicalement [votre oncle] est mort, juridiquement il est absent').[28] To cover the

25 'a suspenseful, humorous film'.
26 'a slight, innocent, film; a modest entertainment of little real interest'.
27 'secret hiding-place'.

costs of upkeep that will be incurred by the castle during this period, the cousins start organising a *son et lumière* spectacle based on the castle's legend, according to which their ancestor Simon de Kéraudren ignored his beautiful young wife Eliane in favour of his passion for hunting, she took a lover, and then threw herself from the castle's tower when Simon returned early from the hunt one day and surprised her with Gilles. But as the *son et lumière* takes shape, inexplicable deaths start to occur among them: Henri is electrocuted as he tests out the enormous floodlights that will illuminate the castle, and André is killed by an unknown hand, apparently on account of the affair he has been conducting with another married cousin, Jeanne. Finally, in a moment of high drama during the dress rehearsal for the *son et lumière* show, Jeanne – who is of frail and suggestible mind and has been tormented for days by voices telling her she is responsible for her lover's death, and that her destiny is to take her own life like the unfaithful Eliane – jumps from the tower in front of the assembled audience, in a perfect re-enactment of the castle's legend. (The voice Jeanne has heard was in fact real and was that of the murderer in the cousins' midst, talking through the loudspeakers installed in each room of the castle for the historical tour accompanying the *son et lumière*.) In the closing section of the film, Jean-Marie (Jean-Louis Trintignant) and Edwige (Marianne Koch) set a trap to catch the murderer by staging a riding accident for Edwige that leaves her on a respirator and vulnerable to foul play. When cousin Guillaume enters her room during the second evening's *son et lumière* performance and switches off her respirator, she slowly lifts off the domed plastic bubble encasing her in oxygenated air, just as (to Guillaume's horrified amazement) Jean-Marie emerges from the wardrobe to pronounce knowingly 'Ah, c'était vous l'assassin!'.[29] Guillaume bolts for his freedom, but is stopped in his tracks at the castle gate by a bullet expertly fired into his leg from the window of Edwige's room by the only other surviving cousin, Christian. In the chase leading up to this denouement the secret hiding-place enclosing the Comte's dead body has been accidentally revealed, so that his funeral can now take place and the inheritance be dispensed and organised. Jean-Marie, Edwige and Christian are the only cousin-heirs left to attend the funeral, a scene which became the film's most remarked-upon set piece – a

28 'Medically speaking your uncle is dead, juridically speaking he is absent'.
29 'Ah, you were the murderer!'

procession in traditional Breton costume through the Carnac standing stones, to the accompaniment of Georges Brassens' song 'Les Funérailles d'antan' issuing from a transistor radio held by Jean-Marie's girlfriend Micheline (Dany Saval), a key character in the film despite consistently being excluded from 'family' affairs at the castle.

Pleins feux sur l'assassin therefore conforms to the 'polar' in its plot, which is a mixture of a conventional thriller and an Agatha-Christie-style country-house murder mystery, but also contains many elements that do not fit the genre – instances of horror (an owl attacks Jeanne on the staircase to the tower in a moment uncannily prefiguring Hitchcock's 1963 *The Birds*), many flashes of humour (the closing funeral scene; a fat, flat-footed frogman employed to dive the castle moat to locate the Comte's body), and an unmistakably self-aware reflection on 'spectacle' in the way the *son et lumière* is woven into the film's narrative, overlapping with the action at key moments (Jeanne's suicide, the eventual apprehension of Guillaume, who almost manages to escape through the show's midst by passing as a performer). In principle a *son et lumière* is a spectacular theatre of emptiness that operates through sound and suggestion and involves no embodied actors, so the moments at which the bodies of Jeanne and Guillaume appear *in* the spectacle transgress its rules, marking a coincidence of representation and bodily reality that explodes the opposition between the two by revealing 'reality' to be pervasively constructed by (spectacular) representation. The centrality of the *son et lumière* to the overall narrative of *Pleins feux* reinforces this deconstruction of the opposition between representation and the 'real'.

Many reviewers remarked that *Pleins feux* was atypical as a 'polar' or suspense thriller (*Les Arts* 12 April 1961; *France-soir* 6 April 1961; *Libération* 6 October 1992): the generic puzzle it poses is perhaps best summarised by François Chevassu, who described the film as 'fort difficile à classer, film policier sans doute, mais aussi film d'épouvante, film burlesque, film spectacle avec le son et lumière, film polyvalent, un peu trop sans doute' (Chevassu 1961).[30] Critical opinion was unanimous that Franju was not at all interested in his characters, who are two-dimensional constructs subordinate to everything else going on in the film. One 1961 reviewer picked on the *son et lumière* as the

---

30 'extremely hard to classify, a thriller, undoubtedly, but also a horror film, a burlesque, a "spectacle" film, a multifunctional film, probably a bit too much'.

'true' subject of *Pleins feux* (Gilbert Guez, *Les Arts* 15 March 1961), and a re-evaluation of the film offered by *Cahiers du cinéma* (Magny 1992) on the occasion of its 1992 re-release (the print had been 'lost' and the film unviewed for the intervening thirty years (Maison de la Villette 1992: 133)) also pursues this line of argument. In this article, Joël Magny identifies the *son et lumière* as the start of a *mise en abyme* in the film (1992: 48), a feature he suggests may be read as indicative of Franju's modernity.[31] Whereas 1960s reviewers tended to see Franju as having ruined the coherence of his film by taking his rather ordinary material too seriously, and overloading it with knowing cinephile gags (*Le Figaro* 9 April 1961), Magny insists that Franju's cleverness is modern and subversive. A commentator for *Libre Belgique* in 1962 did notice what is probably the best example of reflexive comment upon representation in *Pleins feux*, which occurs during the only scene of intimacy between Jeanne and André. Their conversation ends abruptly when Jeanne retreats into her dressing-room from fear of the deafening claps of thunder coming from outside the castle, but André then throws open her room's shutters to reveal a sound rehearsal for the *son et lumière* in progress outside – in other words, Franju knowingly mocks any spectatorial identification with Jeanne's fear in advance of the deluded self-defenestration it will lead to later.

Initial impressions that *Pleins feux sur l'assassin* was a 'pantalon rapiécé, fait de tapons et de morceaux'[32] (*La Croix* 21 April 1961) have proved extremely hard to dislodge. *Le Monde*'s critic Jean de Baroncelli suggested that in his third feature film Franju was still casting about for the cinematic genre that suited him and would allow him to express his 'personal poetry' (*Le Monde* 6 April 1961). I hope to be making it clear by now that, in my view, Franju's *long métrage* cinema was not destined for and would never have fitted in any single genre, and indeed needed to range across generic codings in order to communicate the plethora of images Franju had to express. The superb, elegant décors and photography of *Pleins feux sur l'assassin* are the one aspect of the film which cannot fail to impress: it was shot entirely on

31 'Bien avant d'autres cinéastes "modernes", de Rossellini à Schroeter, entre autres, Franju a l'intuition que le cinéma n'a plus à filmer que du "déjà-en-représentation"' ('Well before other "modern" directors from Rossellini to Schroeter, Franju had the insight that cinema should be filming self-reflexively') (Magny 1992: 50).

32 'patched-together pair of trousers, made of bits and pieces'.

location at the chateau de Bretesche in Brittany, with additional
interiors filmed at the neighbouring chateau of Goulaine. Franju's
conception of *Pleins feux sur l'assassin* depended on its castle setting:
he visited dozens of Breton chateaux before finding a suitable one,
and from the first saw the chateau not simply as *a* character in the
film but as its chief character (Bellour and Lacassin 1961). The only
reviewer to recognise that *mise-en-scène* was Franju's overriding
motive for and interest in making *Pleins feux* was Michel Delahaye
writing in *Cahiers du cinéma*, who summarised the issue as follows:
'Etant donné un château, que faire en ce château? Tout, s'est dit
Franju, ce qu'on peut faire en ce château'[33] (Delahaye 1961: 61) – even
if this 'tout' proves ultimately not to be enough to compensate for the
film's other shortcomings.

Other echoes: *film noir* and melodrama

At the start of this chapter I suggested a parallel between Franju's
early features and those of Godard and Chabrol, in whose films the
generic marks of gangster movies, the musical and the thriller abound.
The early years of the *nouvelle vague* were extraordinarily rich in
influences from American genre cinema and, despite his aloofness
from the *Cahiers* directors, these appear in Franju's cinema as they do
in Godard's and Chabrol's, in the form of the marks of *film noir* and
melodrama. In this section I shall look first at *film noir*, by referring to
theoretical discussions that have guided recent research into this
cinematic area, and by tracing the *noir* elements to be found in
Franju's first five features (*La Tête contre les murs* to *Judex*).

    As Pam Cook points out in her summary of *noir* criticism, 'the
crucial issue, as phrased by Silver and Ward, is that of 'cohesiveness':
the wide influence of noir *across* the work of different directors and
genres' (Cook 1985: 93). There is of course an original period of and
location for *film noir*, which is from 1941 to 1958 in Hollywood (Cook
1985: 93), but recently critics have preferred to open up this original
body of work, to explore its prehistory and afterlife, and to affirm the
existence of *noir* in other national traditions, particularly that of

33 'Given a castle, what does one do in it? Everything, replies Franju, that can be
   done in a castle'.

France, whose 1930s poetic realists are now regarded by some as its originators. Early criticism of *film noir* saw it as a genre tied to a specific period and location, but the looser term 'movement' was quickly preferred (Durgnat 1996; Place 1996; Schrader 1996), a change paralleled by a shift in the object of critical enquiry from subject matter (character, milieu and plot) to visual style. As Sylvia Harvey explains,

> The defining contours of this group of films are the product of that which is abnormal and dissonant. And the dissonances, the sense of disorientation and unease, while frequently present at the level of plot and thematic development are, more importantly perhaps, always a function of the visual style of this group of films. (Harvey 1978: 35)

Since the term *film noir* was initially derived from 'série noire' literature of the type used by Franju in *Les Yeux sans visage*, *Pleins feux sur l'assassin* and his homages to Feuillade, his affinity with the movement is evident, and horror and fantasy are, as Durgnat puts it, 'first cousins to the *film noir*' (Durgnat 1996: 50). Franju's links to *film noir*, reinforced by the emphasis on visual style now dominant in *noir* criticism, are manifold, and a discussion of them is long overdue.[34] My exploration of the *noir* elements in Franju's early features will concentrate on two aspects: the theme of criminals and criminality, and the visual marks of *noir* – chiaroscuro and low-key lighting, the pervasiveness of the dark and shadows, and the prevalent atmospheres of claustrophobia and despair. Since I have already discussed *Pleins feux sur l'assassin* and *Judex* in detail in this chapter, I shall base the discussion on *La Tête contre les murs* and *Thérèse Desqueyroux*, taking in *Les Yeux sans visage* because of its compelling illustration of some central features of *noir*.

In *La Tête contre les murs*, *Les Yeux sans visage* and *Thérèse Desqueyroux*, all the main protagonists are criminals. Although the social settings of a psychiatric hospital, a clinic and a bourgeois estate have nothing in common with the gangster milieux of classic French *noir* films such as Jean Becker's *Touchez pas au grisbi* and Jules Dassin's *Du rififi chez les hommes*, François Gérane, Genessier and his assistant Louisa, and Thérèse Desqueyroux herself commit and are punished

---

34 Robin Buss includes no fewer than four of Franju's features in the filmography of his book *French Film Noir*, 'One hundred and one French *films noirs*', but devotes only a short discussion to one of them, *Judex*, in the main body of his book (1994: 86).

for robbery and assault, abduction and unauthorised medical experimentation, and poisoning respectively. François Gérane is a petty criminal who steals from and burns important papers belonging to his lawyer-father: his rebellious and anti-social behaviour is responded to as full-scale delinquency and 'treated' with all the punitive force the medical institution can muster when he is interned in a psychiatric hospital from which he will never be discharged. In *Les Yeux sans visage*, Genessier shows frightening cruelty in his treatment of the young girls he abducts and his 'experimental' dogs, and yet manages to be a sympathetic wrongdoer, since it is desperation and love for his daughter Christiane that drives him to these criminal acts. Thérèse Desqueyroux, similarly, plots to kill her husband Bernard in order to be free of the suffocating marriage in which she has become trapped. Thérèse is a prisoner of her class and of her gender; the stealthy acts of poisoning depicted in Mauriac's novel are what contemporary psychology would call a 'cry for help', and the 'non-lieu' pronounced at Thérèse's trial and eventual compassion shown by Bernard seem to indicate awareness of this, even if Thérèse remains an enigma to her husband until the end.

Various elements in the portrayal of these four characters enable an assessment of how prevalent *noir* criminality and claustrophobia are in each film. In *Thérèse Desqueyroux*, Thérèse eventually regains her freedom when she is allowed to take up residence in Paris as a consequence of the anorexic illness suffered during her period of imposed solitary confinement. An accommodation is reached between Thérèse and the bourgeoisie; she cannot be free of her class since she is still bound to it legally, by marriage, but she regains her intellectual and moral independence as a woman, which considerably attenuates the bleak atmosphere of the entire central part of the film. No such release awaits Genessier and Louisa in *Les Yeux sans visage*, who (in keeping with the film's horror) are stabbed and mauled as punishment for their evil and complicity in crime. Of the three films and all Franju's early features, though, it is *La Tête contre les murs* that conforms most closely to the downward spiral of misfortune and misery characteristic of *film noir*. François Gérane tries repeatedly to escape from the asylum, once on the arm of his girlfriend Stéphanie (Anouk Aimée) at visiting time, once in the company of his timid and sad friend Heurtevent (Charles Aznavour), who is an epileptic and suffers a fit which scuppers their escape attempt, and most dramatically at the end of the film, when he dodges away from Heurtevent's funeral (who has hanged himself out of hopelessness), scales the asylum walls and runs across open fields back to Paris and to Stéphanie. Tellingly for a *noir* hero, however, François goes to the very place where he is certain to be caught; Stéphanie covers for him once when anonymous agents call to reintern him, but François leaves her apartment shortly afterwards, foolishly believing he can manage alone, and is instantly caught by the same agents waiting on the staircase. The final shots of the film exactly repeat the earlier sequence in which François is first sequestered, as the ambulance transporting him races along the asylum walls in the darkness, a terrible vision of imminent imprisonment and despair.

Since *film noir* so often depicts criminals and criminal activity, sympathy for the perpetrators of crime is almost a prerequisite of the style. The four protagonists I have just discussed are common criminals, not gangsters; their wrongdoing is accounted for by situation and circumstance rather than being motivated by a desire for wealth or power. Genessier and Louisa are comprehensible rather than endearing, but François Gérane and Thérèse Desqueyroux are highly sympathetic criminals, and reveal a real interest in criminal psychology on Franju's part. (The same cannot be said of *Pleins feux sur l'assassin* and *Judex*, where psychology takes a definite second place to *mise-en-scène*; the catwoman Diana Monti can be seen as a similar archetype of *film noir* to the spiderwoman discussed by Place (1996), but like the murderer of *Pleins feux sur l'assassin* is given no psychological depth.) A further aspect of the *noir* criminality of Franju's early features relates to the claim made by Sylvia Harvey that *film noir* is 'structured around the destruction or absence of romantic love and the family' (Harvey 1978: 37). The crimes and misdemeanours of Gérane, Genessier and Louise, and Thérèse all relate to their roles as family members; François is a 'delinquent' son, Genessier a dominating and guilty father, and Thérèse a depressed and desperate wife. The role played by family structures in these three films is an issue I shall discuss more fully in Chapter 4, but the relationship perceived by feminist critics between *film noir* and issues of gender and the family make it worth an advance mention here.

Visual style is probably even more important than the theme of criminality in creating *noir* atmospheres in these three films, and although their locations are predominantly suburban and rural rather than urban, continuous use is made of scenes shot at night, shadow, and chiaroscuro lighting effects. In *Thérèse Desqueyroux*, the monotonous landscapes of the Landes region often signify Thérèse's sense of imprisonment in her marriage, as a counterpoint to which skies are filmed for the variety of atmospheres they can suggest: the film opens with a long pan round a leaden sky accompanied by a mournful section of Maurice Jarre's music. Since the film is in black and white, luminosity and darkness are the main qualities the sky can convey, and at different points, rapid vertical tracking shots upwards from trees to glowering skies suggest Thérèse's desperate search for relief and freedom.

In *Les Yeux sans visage* there are some stark contrasts of lighting between adjacent scenes, for example between the low-ceilinged, brightly lit interior of the operating theatre and the gloomy roominess of the rest of Dr Genessier's villa. The white walls and white uniforms of Genessier's clinic, adjacent to his suburban villa, provide occasional gleaming (albeit cold and sinister) relief from the shadowy claustrophobia that prevails in the film, and is most directly perceptible in the villa's garage, where Genessier's luxury DS and Louisa's 2CV lie eerily side by side, and on its staircases, where Christiane's inquisitive wanderings inform her of her father's illicit activities. In the scene where Genessier and Louisa carry the abducted and chloroformed Edna to the blockhouse for surgery, the bannisters of the staircase cast ominous cage-like shadows everywhere, exactly as the bars of real cages do in the scene where Christiane visits Genessier's dogs' pound in order to offer them comfort. As Louisa lures Edna away from the Latin quarter of Paris by offering her the room she is seeking, she casts a dark shadow on the café wall behind her, and when the plot to expose Genessier is running its course towards the end of the film, he casts huge shadows on the white walls of his clinic. Most striking of all in Franju's exploitation of 'shadow symbolism' is the early scene in which Genessier deliberately misidentifies the body of his first surgery-victim as Christiane's in order to end society's curiosity about the aftermath of the accident that has disfigured her. Here, the camera dollies forward through the gloomy corridors of the police station into the 'Identification Room' (Salle de Reconnaissance) and up to the body-bearing trolley, the only lit object in a room whose walls are covered by the shadows of grilles and of its occupants. The atmosphere of this sequence is one of utter blackness and corruption;

Genessier arrives and leaves in the dark, just as the two desperate trips to dump the bodies of his and Louisa's victims – one to the river, the second to the echoing family vault in the graveyard – are made at night. When the police 'plant' Paulette Mérodon leaves the clinic after an apparently unsuccessful attempt to expose Genessier's traffic in young blonde girls, it is during the pitch blackness of her fifteen-minute walk to the Paris bus that she is approached and abducted back to the villa by Louisa.

Central to the creation of sinister *noir* atmospheres in Franju's first two features is the contribution of his German-born director of photography, Eugen Shuftan. A contemporary of Fritz Lang's, Shuftan worked in German silent cinema and extensively in Hollywood from the 1920s on, often on fantasy films or films featuring crime. Even more importantly, he was a leading director of lighting and photography for the poetic realists of late 1930s France, where his signature mastery of mystery and gloom was employed by Marcel Carné on *Drôle de drame ou l'étrange aventure de Docteur Molyneux* (1937) and *Quai des brumes* (1938). Shuftan worked, in other words, at the heart of the two European cinema movements that may legitimately be regarded as precursors of American *film noir*. Since he first worked with Franju on *La Première Nuit* in 1958, his involvement in Franju's cinema was brief, but his influence on the brooding and pessimistic style of *La Tête contre les murs* and *Les Yeux sans visage* is unmistakable.

La Tête contre les murs' conformity with *noir* in terms of plot and psychology is only furthered by the quantity of scenes shot at night and by Franju's exploitation of chiaroscuro. After François meets Stéphanie in the opening scene, they arrive back in Paris to darkness relieved only by gleams of light reflected from their leather jackets and the expensive cars belonging to François's 'friends'. The party they attend briefly is on a houseboat on the Seine, and in a striking use of high contrast white-on-black filming, a (white) girl in a white bikini swims out of the pitch black water back to the houseboat, where she flirts with François on her way in. The entire opening sequence of François's vandalism against his father is shot at night, with the only non-artificial lighting provided by the lamp of François' motorbike and a candlestick he uses to light his way into his father's study and to burn the legal papers he knows should not be in his father's private possession. After his father has telephoned the order to have his son committed to a psychiatric hospital, François' terrifying ride to the asylum is figured just by the headlights of the ambulance car racing along the institution's walls (a shot repeated at the film's conclusion, as I noted above). And in this first part of *La Tête contre les murs*, it is not only darkness and shadow that convey the dissonance and disorientation so characteristic of *film noir*; in the opening credits sequence François displays his 'motocross' skills by riding his motorbike in swooping diagonals and vertical plunges across that cut up each shot and render balanced framing completely impossible. The film is launched in a frenzied atmosphere of speed and confusion powerfully anticipatory both of François' situation and the *noir* mood that will prevail throughout.

Although many of the scenes in the asylum take place in daylight, darkness seems to be waiting to threaten François outside the walls; his first escape attempt with Heurtevent takes place at twilight, their two dark figures scurrying away from the powerful torches wielded by Docteur Varmont and his assistants. As in *Les Yeux sans visage*, darkness is sometimes used in a straightforwardly symbolic fashion; the only exterior shot of the asylum at night occurs just after Heurtevent's suicide, and on one or two occasions sunshine and bright skies seem to represent hope – if only in contrast to dark woods in the asylum's grounds and the trench of Heurtevent's grave. Shadows of the human figure also appear at suggestive moments, such as the eerie scene in which Docteur Varmont injects François with a sedative while eliciting from him his account of his mother's death (Varmont's large menacing shadow is cast on the wall of the consulting room), and on the staircase to Stéphanie's flat in the penultimate scene, where officials wait in the gloom to pounce on a François over-confident of his freedom; the looming black shadow François casts as he descends the stairs seems to figure his entire unfree self, his past and his future. The closing scenes of *La Tête contre les murs* take place at night and in the dark just like its opening part, completing a circle of confinement characteristic of the most claustrophobic and doom-laden *film noir*. As is shown by his anguished face and hands gripping the bars of the ambulance car, for François, there has been and will be no escape.

There are, then, unmistakable currents of *noir* running through Franju's early feature films, and in *La Tête contre les murs* it is more strongly marked than any other genre, in my view strongly enough to call the drama full-scale *film noir*. My contention that the genre influences in Franju's cinema may be understood as parallel to the visible influence of American genre cinema on the directors of the *nouvelle vague* is only strengthened when it comes to melodrama, whose traces are unmissable in all Franju's films of the same five-year period except *La Tête contre les murs*. In order to discuss the part played by melodrama in these films I shall first make a detour via another Franju production, the last film of his working life and one shot for and shown only on television, *Le Dernier Mélodrame* (1978).

As its title suggests, *Le Dernier Mélodrame* is a story that explicitly thematises the characteristics and qualities of melodrama – theatrical melodrama, a staple of nineteenth- and early twentieth-century theatre all but killed off by the international rise of television in the 1960s, and the subsequent explosion in television soap opera. Franju's film depicts this decline by portraying the self-destructive end of a small travelling theatre troupe (its impresario mounts the stage of his burning theatre, set alight by a jealous arsonist, and expires among the ruins): it is 'une sorte de réflexion sur le théâtre et le spectacle en général' (Schlockoff 1979: 70).[35] The idea for *Le Dernier Mélodrame* was originally suggested to Franju by Pierre Brasseur in 1964, but it was not until 1976 that an offer from the French television station FR3 gave him the chance to make it (Beylie 1978: 29). The subject provided the opportunity to develop reflections on representation, theatricality and spectacle that had already figured in different ways in Franju's cinema in *Pleins feux sur l'assassin, Judex* and *Thomas l'imposteur*. What attracted Franju particularly to melodrama was its foregrounding of theatricalised emotion, or as he put it, 'impudeur' and 'mensonge'[36] (Beylie and Schapira 1984: 11), qualities that can immediately be seen in the pulp and picaresque narratives of *Les Yeux sans visage, Pleins feux sur l'assassin* and *Judex*. Franju's attraction to the melodramatic overlaps significantly with his emotional investment in stories of murder, mystery and adventure, even if it is not exactly the same thing.

Melodrama tugs on the emotions, and according to Franju appeals directly to our taste for misfortune and unhappiness (Beylie and Schapira 1984: 11). More specifically, according to recent film theory, it often depends on the presence of a victim or victims who is/are usually female (Cook 1985: 74; Mulvey 1989). Franju seems to have

---

35 'a sort of reflexion on theatre and spectacle in general'.
36 'immodesty' and 'deceit'.

been aware of this aspect of melodramatic narrative in advance of its 'discovery' by 1970s feminist film writings, since he commented in 1975 that whereas he had always seen *Judex* as 'une féerie mélodramatique'[37] (Brumagne 1977: 16), *Nuits rouges* (his other homage to Feuillade) did not merit the term 'since there is no fluttering victim and therefore no melodrama' (Milne 1975: 69). In *Le Dernier Mélodrame* the theatre is destroyed by the men of the town who rise up because their womenfolk's lives have been taken over by the sentimental and escapist stories they have been watching on its stage: in this catastrophic scenario neither gender ultimately suffers more than the other, but men and women are clearly differently positioned in relation to theatricality and emotion; gender is a key element in propelling the narrative. In Franju's earlier features, though, a 'fluttering victim' is precisely the element mainly responsible for lending the films their melodramatic narrative and images, and with this in view I shall briefly discuss how these elements are manifested in *Les Yeux sans visage*, *Pleins feux sur l'assassin*, and *Judex* (since Thérèse's identity as victim of bourgeois patriarchy has already figured in my discussion of *film noir*, I shall leave aside *Thérèse Desqueyroux*).

All three of these films feature a fragile woman in need of protection and rescue. In *Pleins feux sur l'assassin*, Jeanne's neurotic susceptibility to persecution (the murderer repeatedly reminds her of her identification through adulterous guilt with the ill-fated heroine of the castle's legend) and theatrical suicide is only one micronarrative in a sequence of orchestrated deaths, but in *Les Yeux sans visage* and *Judex* Christiane's mistreatment and Jacqueline's need for protection are fundamental to the films' narratives. Separated from her fiancé and denied any social existence when Genessier uses the body of his first surgical victim to fake her funeral, Christiane is often seen lying prostrate on the chaise longue in the villa's sitting room, unable to face what her life has become and unwilling to wear the mask that protects others from her disfigurement and suffering. On several occasions she pleads to be allowed to take her own life, the fate that actually overtakes the film's third female victim, Edna Grüberg. After the operation to transplant Edna's face onto Christiane, and Edna's suicide, the narrative proceeds more quietly for some time, but when a fourth potential victim has been lured to the surgery and the

37 'a melodramatic fantasy'.

police investigation is putting pressure on events at Genessier's clinic, it erupts again into the extraordinarily melodramatic scenes of Christiane's revolt. Starting with a mute shake of her head, Christiane cuts free the police 'plant' Paulette Mérodon from the operating table with a surgical scalpel, approaches her father's assistant Louisa, whom she stabs once in the neck with the same instrument, then moves swiftly to free her father's dogs from their cages. The penultimate images of the film show Genessier on the ground, mauled by his overjoyed and vengeful animals, his cruel and misguided reign over his family finally at an end.

In *Judex* the image of the fragile, innocent daughter-victim is incarnated even more completely by Jacqueline, who plays an entirely passive role in the narrative until Judex–Vallières (it is by means of his disguise as the doddering but protective family butler Vallières that Judex comes to care for her) finally vanquishes the scheming Diana Monti. When Jacqueline discovers after her father Favraux's apparent death that he is a ruthless scoundrel, she renounces her inheritance and leaves the family property to live a quiet life with her daughter, an indication of true goodness and virtue. Adventure pursues her, however, and she is twice kidnapped and narrowly escapes death – from drowning in the river where Diana and her accomplice dump her drugged body, and from stabbing at Diana's hand when the two villains imprison her in the old mill (Judex arrives just before the knife goes in, even if he fails to trap Diana on this occasion). The images in the sequences of Jacqueline's kidnappings are more melodramatic and poetic than most in a film brimming with them; she is assailed with a hypodermic syringe by a Diana disguised as a nun, and floats unconscious down a fast-flowing river with only her face (inexplicably and miraculously) remaining above water.

In both *Les Yeux sans visage* and *Judex*, then, melodramatic action is usually linked to images of passive and victimised femininity, with all the pathos to which this gives rise. But the identification that enables the spectator to feel the entrapment, despair and panic suffered by Christiane and Jacqueline is also produced by the very person and figure of the actress who plays these parts, Edith Scob. The peculiar delicacy of Scob's features and the fragility of her body are instrumental in producing the melodrama of Franju's early films, because she elicits a highly ambivalent protectiveness from the spectator of which Franju was well aware:

Melodrama consists in giving people the sense of drama – making them want a drama to happen. And, as soon as we want a drama, where have our better feelings gone? As soon as we want to protect the unfortunate heroine, we must first want her to be unfortunate. That's why I say melodrama is utter hypocrisy. But I also say that melodrama has its truth. It brings us as close as possible. It was popular because it was sentimental and public. (Brown 1983: 267)

The obverse of the protectiveness aroused by Scob is desire, both possessive desire for her and a desire that adverse circumstances befall her, a relationship with female victimhood that is the key dynamic in the melodramatic narratives of Franju's early films. Franju's own involvement with melodrama is perhaps best summarised by what he once said about his close and doubtless desiring (though never sexual) relationship with Scob, which is that she was not an inspiration to his film-making but a kindred spirit, an embodiment of magic and fragility he was lucky enough to meet after she gained a small role as an asylum inmate in *La Tête contre les murs*. His sense upon meeting her was of recognition, not of novelty; her appearance was the projection incarnate of a part of him (Maison de la Villette 1992: 70).

Translating literary classics: Franju's adaptations of *Thérèse Desqueyroux*, *Thomas l'Imposteur* and *La Faute de l'Abbé Mouret*

As mentioned earlier in this chapter, there are three 'true' literary adaptations among Franju's eight *longs métrages*. (Although *La Tête contre les murs* and *Les Yeux sans visage* are drawn from Hervé Bazin's *La Tête contre les murs* and Jean Redon's *Celle qui n'était plus* respectively, the relationship between the source novel and Franju's film is a loose one of inspiration rather than one of intended 'translation' from novel to screen.) In this final section of the chapter, I shall discuss *Thérèse Desqueyroux* (from François Mauriac), *Thomas l'Imposteur* (from Jean Cocteau), and *La Faute de l'Abbé Mouret* (from Emile Zola) as the full-scale adaptations they are, relating them to the dominant theories of adapting literary works for the screen, and setting them in the context of their period, which is from 1962 to 1970.

In his classic volume of criticism *Film and Literature*, Morris Beja summarises what he calls the 'two basic approaches to the whole question of adaptation' as follows:

The first approach asks that the integrity of the original work ... be preserved, and therefore that it should not be tampered with and should in fact be uppermost in the preserver's mind. The second approach feels it proper and in fact necessary to adapt the original work freely, in order to create – in the different medium that is now being employed – a new, different work of art with its own integrity. (Beja 1976: 82)

More recent approaches to adaptation have not been dominated to the same degree by what might be termed 'the fidelity problem', since in French cinema of the 1980s and 1990s the issue has been subsumed to a large extent into debates about 'heritage cinema', the exploitation in film of national cultural capital, which often includes classic literary texts. During the 1960s, however, fidelity to the source text was still a central question. The two approaches outlined by Beja constitute a binary opposition between fidelity and freedom (or 'creativity') that is in fact entirely eluded by Franju's three adaptations, which are both highly faithful to their source texts and alive to what the medium of film can bring to the particular narrative involved. Rather than an 'either/or' response to the stark choice of adaptation strategies summarised by Beja, in other words, they offer a 'both/and' solution to the opposition of fidelity to cinematic creativity. Critical assessments of the success of their creativity differ, as might be expected, but there has never been any noteworthy disagreement among reviewers and critics about the accuracy with which Franju transposed his chosen literary narratives into the medium of film.

The other bias dominating thinking about adaptation in the 1960s was that in the wake of the *nouvelle vague*, it was frowned upon by many as an unoriginal, uninventive kind of film-making. François Truffaut's 1954 article 'Une certaine tendance du cinéma français', hugely influential in preparing a culture that would welcome his films and those of other *Cahiers* directors at the end of the 1950s, had focused almost exclusively on attacking the scriptwriters and adapters Aurenche and Bost, and on criticising French feature film-making of the 1950s as dominated by expensive literary adaptations, and therefore devoid of original material, innovative cinematic practices, or the voices of (youthful) *auteurs*. As I suggested in my introduction, Franju differed from the *auteur* model set out by Truffaut: for Franju a literary adaptation was no less personal than writing one's own story, and Renoir would not have been a greater *auteur* in Franju's eyes if he had not adapted *Madame Bovary* and other classic novels (Brumagne 1977: 60, 69).

In turning to literary adaptation in 1962 with *Thérèse Desqueyroux*, then, Franju was going against the grain, but it was a grain he had never particularly wanted or tried to follow, despite cordial relations with *Cahiers du cinéma* and the admiration expressed by Truffaut and Godard for his first two features. *Thérèse Desqueyroux* in fact constitutes a kind of exception among Franju's adaptations, in that it was a project that appears to have emerged only shortly before he undertook it (*Thomas l'Imposteur* and *La Faute de l'Abbé Mouret* were both novels he had wanted to film for many years). But in another vital respect it resembles the two later films – its depiction of an institution or phenomenon onto which Franju could bring to bear the corruscating social criticism demonstrated in many of his documentaries. *Thomas l'Imposteur* contains a devastating critique of war, and is a counterpart to *Hôtel des Invalides*; *La Faute de l'Abbé Mouret*, finally shot in 1970, gives full voice to the anti-clerical views Franju had often expressed during previous decades. In the unanticipated *Thérèse Desqueyroux*, the target is the money- and family-obsessed bourgeoisie of the Landes region of the southwest of France, the region and class from which Mauriac came and which is depicted in the same terms in his novel, first published in 1927. Franju's three adaptations of novels can therefore be classed together by content, and not only as adaptations. They constitute a separate strand of his film-making from his five other *longs métrages*, although the strand may overlap slightly with the acute and arguably critical observation of the psychiatric asylum in *La Tête contre les murs*.

Despite its unfashionableness, *Thérèse Desqueyroux* was greeted with almost universal acclaim by the French press, and favourably compared with recent adaptations of Balzac, Stendhal and Hugo (*Combat* 27 September 1962).[38] It represented France at the Venice film festival, where it narrowly missed carrying off the Lion d'Or, and where Emmanuelle Riva won the award for best actress (*Les Lettres françaises* 29 August 1962 and 4 October 1962). The film was received not as a product of its very modern moment, but as a classic novel – probably Mauriac's best known, and the only one adapted for the cinema – transposed to the screen in classic style (*Arts* 2 October

---

38 Only *Positif*'s critic M. Ranchal disliked the film (and intensely), because (by his own admission) it did not conform to the kind of cinema he and his colleagues had expected and hoped for from Franju (*Positif* 49 (1962): 77). Writing for *Cahiers du cinéma*, Claude Beylie gave the film an extremely positive review.

1962; *Le Co-opérateur de France* 3 October 1962). Apart from the occasional jibe at excessive fidelity to Mauriac's text and the 'poetics' of the novel's settings (*Europe* 1 February 1963), critics all praised the exactitude of its rendering of Thérèse's story, and its 'honesty' (*Le Canard enchaîné* 29 September 1962). Given the importance of locale and atmosphere to the novel – the property-owning bourgeoisie and oppressively tall pine forests of the Landes – and the success of the film in conveying these (it was shot on location in houses found by Franju in the Villandraut region which closely matched those described in the novel), there can be no doubt that 'added value' was produced by the visual medium; in other words, that Franju had avoided the technique of mere 'equivalences' to scenes in the novel practised by Aurenche and Bost and pilloried by Truffaut in 1954.

Only a few changes from Mauriac's text were noted by reviewers in the film, the most important of which is certainly the omission of any of the Catholic significance seen in the novel by its author. For Mauriac, Thérèse was guilty of the sin of pride, through believing herself superior to Bernard Desqueyroux and her class of origin, an angle on his own material borne out by the later novel *La Fin de la nuit*, in which he returned to the character of Thérèse and 'punished' her for the earlier crime the courts had not convicted her for – largely because of Bernard's failure to testify against her, due to his fear of scandal. Franju on the other hand, as a staunch non-believer, went on record as saying that he believed in and supported Thérèse's struggle for freedom from Argelouse and the bourgeoisie of the southwest, and considered a sequel undesirable.[39] As a consequence, his film does not linger on or develop any of the instances where a religious interpretation seemed most possible, such as the moment of 'divine intervention' when Thérèse is prevented from swallowing poison by news of the death of 'tante Clara'.

The second shift between Mauriac's and Franju's *Thérèse Desqueyroux* is Franju's updating of the story, set in the late 1920s, to the 1960s. This entailed a rewriting of the dialogue spoken by the character of Jean Azévédo, Anne's would-be lover who quits Argelouse some time before Thérèse is finally able to: in Franju's film, the intellectual passion that connects her to him when they eventually meet is not René Bazin, but the theatre of Chekhov. Franju claimed that moving

39 'Je n'envisage pas une suite à cette fin qui lui laisse l'espoir' ('I don't envisage a sequel to the ending that gives her a chance') (Buache 1962).

the action of Mauriac's novel forward by 35 years mattered little because the provincial class and locale depicted remained essentially unchanged, a powerful argument (Buache 1962: 14). Perhaps the strongest points against it are Durgnat's questions about the alternatives to a stifling domestic existence that would have been available to Thérèse in 1962, though not in 1927 – the company of other young people, music, mobility (Durgnat 1967: 96). In other respects, Franju turns details of modernisation to his advantage, a good example being the changed form of transport in which Thérèse travels back from her trial to face Bernard – a car rather than a train and a coach, whose window serves as a conveniently private screen for the projection of Thérèse's memories during the sequence of flashbacks (accompanied by her interior monologue) that constitutes the entire first half of the film. Despite accusing Franju of 'psychological archaism', Durgnat then concedes that the issue is ultimately of limited importance: 'by the time Franju's film is forty years old (2003) ... the film's anachronisms will have faded into the background, where they belong' (Durgnat 1967: 96–7).

The anecdote accompanying the story of how Franju came to film Cocteau's *Thomas l'Imposteur* is a commentary on the straitjacket of fidelity against which adaptations were viewed in the postwar period: when Cocteau entrusted his novel (published long before, in 1923) to Franju in 1952, after seeing *Hôtel des Invalides*, he declared 'Je te donne *Thomas*. C'est par toi que je veux être trahi.'[40] It was not until the mid 1960s, however, when Franju had directed five features, that a producer was found to undertake the project: as with *Thérèse Desqueyroux*, potential producers were unconvinced that a novel that had never been transposed to the screen was really worth adapting, and the wartime scenes required by *Thomas l'Imposteur* threatened to consume a considerable budget (*Arts* 9 December 1964). Although Cocteau was jointly credited (with Raphaël Cluzel) for dialogues drawn directly from his novel, he was dead by the time Franju began shooting in 1964, and the film turned into something of a homage to him. But despite the criticisms Franju's *Thomas l'Imposteur* received from some quarters, it is likely Cocteau would have approved of the film, because of the convincing and often terrible portrayal of war on which Franju particularly focused: the story of Cocteau's novel was

40 'I give you *Thomas*. It's you I want to be betrayed by.'

based on his own experience as the organiser of a convoy of ambulance vehicles to the Front during the Great War, the role assumed in his book by the Princesse de Bormes (Buache 1996: 55).

Adapting Cocteau's novel posed enormous challenges, because of the characteristically energetic, buoyant and fantastic style of its language ('un miroitement d'écriture cristalline'[41] (Buache 1996: 56)). As Durgnat notes,

> the visual style of Cocteau's films, for which he is quite certainly as responsible as his photographers and art directors, is completely different from his prose style. In Franju's words, 'Cocteau's cinematographic style, whose roots are in German expressionism which he liked very much. ... is the contrary of his written style which is light, musical, decorative, very French, and whose ornament occasionally camouflages the meaning'. (Durgnat 1967: 126–7)

My comments on the visual motifs Franju's *Thomas l'Imposteur* finds to replace linguistic effects that are quite untranslatable literally follow in Chapter 3, as part of my larger consideration of *mise-en-scène* in Franju's films: what I wish to note here about style and (un)translatability is just that its combination of serious anti-war sentiment and playful linguistic virtuosity made Cocteau's *Thomas* particularly suited to that peculiar blend of genres for which Franju was already reputed, 'réalisme fantastique', a generic and stylistic mix that possibly did mean, as Freddy Buache and others noted, that his *Thomas l'Imposteur* resembled *Judex* far more than it resembled *Thérèse Desqueyroux* (Buache 1996: 57; *Le Canard enchaîné* 12 May 1965; *Le Film français* 7 May 1965; *Télérama* 23 May 1965).

One of its resemblances to *Judex* was in fact the target of most of the criticisms Franju's film received from the press – the absence of psychology in its depiction of character, particularly Guillaume de Fontenoy himself (*L'Express* 10 May 1965; *Le Figaro* 9 May 1965; *Le Monde* 12 May 1965). In both novel and film, Guillaume and the Princesse de Bormes are both drawn to participate in war, as Cocteau himself was, by its aesthetic appeal – by the images produced by the 'theatre' of war (a metaphor that recurs in both Cocteau and Franju). But whereas the Princesse breaks through these privileged and politically very dubious sentiments to the 'reality' of war when she sees the bodies of a mother and daughter lying near Reims cathedral

41 'a shimmering, crystalline writing'.

and (because she loves her daughter) decides to return from the Front, Guillaume/Thomas never does. His psychology, expressed socially in his falsely declared identity as the nephew of General de Fontenoy (the act that enables the Princesse's ambulance convoy to get permits to participate in war and Thomas to see action), is an inextricable blend of fiction and fantasy with his 'real' identity as a sixteen-year-old youth from the provinces. Franju's *Thomas l'Imposteur* is faithful to the plot of Cocteau's novel up to Thomas's death, where both text and the film's narrator report '"Une balle, se dit-il. *Je suis perdu si je ne fais pas semblant d'être mort."* / Mais, en lui, la fiction et la réalité ne formaient qu'un. / Guillaume Thomas était mort.'[42] But whereas Cocteau's novel does express this complex interiority of its eponymous hero to some extent, Franju's film does not. The novel's readers are aware from the start that Thomas is a fake, but the film's spectators only discover this along with the other characters in the film. The result is that the success of Patrice Rouleau's performance as Thomas, which was generally appreciated by reviewers, is due mainly to his remarkable physical suitability for the role (his 'baby' face and lanky, ungainly physique). In psychological terms, Emmanuelle Riva's Princesse is by far the more clearly articulated and sympathetic character – and the dominant one in the film (*Le Monde* 12 May 1965).

The other main aspect of Franju's *Thomas l'Imposteur* that reviewers picked out to criticise was the retention – or premeditated inclusion as voiceover – of sections of narration from Cocteau's novel. Although read by Jean Marais, the star of Cocteau's *Orphée* and therefore familiar to the Cocteau enthusiasts that might be making up much of the film's audience, these passages of narration came across as flat, over-literally faithful and uncinematographic (*Combat* 7 May 1965; *La Croix* 15 May 1965; *Le Figaro* 9 May 1965). In this one instance, it seems Franju could be accused of the mechanical carrying-across of prose into the cinema so detested by Truffaut in Aurenche and Bost's adaptations: instead of actually transposing Cocteau's novel, Franju was merely illustrating it, in a kind of uninspired 'lecture-spectacle' (*Combat* 7 May 1965).[43] The compensation for the disappointing commented scenes, however, was a greatly increased and impressive degree of realism in the uncommented ones (*Combat* 7 May 1965).

42 '"A bullet, he thought. *I'm lost if I don't pretend to be dead."* / But in him, fiction and reality were one. / Guillaume Thomas was dead.'
43 'illustrated reading'.

Franju's film insists on the horrors of war repeatedly, in scenes of the destruction of Reims, the ambulance convoy's discovery of combatants so seriously wounded as to be beyond rescue, and the eerily mournful atmosphere of the trenches on the Belgian coast where Thomas is sent after he is exposed as an impostor, where his friend Payot is killed by a stray bullet and Thomas himself meets his death. The 'creativity' Franju brings to Cocteau, in other words, lies in his transformation of the novel into a social document, achieved at the expense of character study. In defence of this artistic licence (when defence was required), Franju insisted that Cocteau had always said that Thomas and the Princesse de Bormes were not unusually rich psychological beings, and that he would like his novel filmed as a 'documentaire réaliste' (*Les Lettres françaises* 6 May 1965). According to Franju, this was because Cocteau had been furious with the blinkered aestheticism of some of the production team on *La Belle et la bête* (*Les Lettres françaises* 6 May 1965). The centrality of 'aesthetic' theatricalised war to Cocteau's novel did not, in other words, preclude a critique of this attitude, and despite Cocteau's own inclination towards it, he was not naïvely blind to the political implications of the stance. Franju's film, characteristically, nailed his colours to the mast: he believed that Cocteau's *Thomas* was, 'au fond',[44] a pacifist book about the Great War, and filmed his adaptation in line with this vision (*Les Lettres françaises* 6 May 1965). In Franju's words, to see war 'sous une forme lyrique'[45] was an aberration (Maison de la Villette 1992: 116).

Thomas l'Imposteur was not successful commercially (*Les Nouvelles littéraires* 15 October 1970), and it was to be five years before Franju made another film. The project in question was at least his other long-cherished adaptation project, Zola's 1875 novel *La Faute de l'Abbé Mouret*, the fifth in the Rougon-Macquart series and a novel Franju had wanted to bring to the screen since 1953. In the 1950s Franju had wanted Gérard Philippe to play the role of the sinning country priest Serge Mouret, but Philippe had declined, convinced that such a part and a subject were controversial enough to put his career at risk. Franju had also proposed to producers an adaptation fully as anti-clerical as might be expected of him, and had been told his critique of the Catholic church was too extreme for audiences of the time (*Les*

44 'at bottom'.
45 'lyrically'.

Nouvelles littéraires 15 October 1970). However, by the end of the 1960s the ecclesiastical climate in France had relaxed to such a point that the self-censorship Franju admitted had been built into his project no longer applied – although when his producer Vera Belmont phoned him to report that the film had finally been accepted, he still reports thinking her call was a joke (*Les Nouvelles littéraires* 15 October 1970). By 1970 the issue of priestly celibacy raised in *La Faute de l'Abbé Mouret* had in fact become a social issue of some importance, since debates about its desirability were in train.

After its release on 14 October 1970 Franju's *La Faute* met with a harsh reception from parts of the the French press. Reviewers criticised its main actors, the 22- year-old Francis Huster in his first film and, in the role of Albine, the relatively unknown Gillian Hills (who had been in Roger Vadim's noted adaptation of Laclos' *Les Liaisons dangereuses* in 1959). Zola's novel is considerably longer than either *Thérèse Desqueyroux* or *Thomas l'Imposteur*, and although Franju respected its plot, he effected several cuts in content, of which the most significant was undoubtedly the omission of the character of Serge Mouret's simple-minded sister Désirée. One reviewer lighted on these changes as giving his film an 'aspect sommaire'[46] (*Actualité* 19 October 1970), and later critics would regret the omission of Désirée's 'happy sunny presence' (Cousins 2001: 69). However, the abbreviation of the novel Franju had to effect in order to fit it into a feature film of a reasonable length (100 minutes) also makes the conflict of views between Mouret and Frère Archangias, his punitive, misogynistic and indeed misanthropic fellow-priest, more dynamic, as does the rearrangement of scenes that brings this contrast of characters into the opening scenes of Franju's film. A third criticism of Franju's adaptation was that it was too explicit, not only in its representation of sexual activity (it opens with a scene of sex in a field between two peasant characters Rosalie and Fortuné, where Zola's novel simply narrates that Rosalie is pregnant by her lover), but in its anti-clericalism (Jacques Siclier said it reduced Christianity to a 'religion and uniform of castrati', *Télérama* 1 November 1970), and in its Biblical symbolism. This last criticism referred particularly to Franju's inclusion (which figures nowhere in the novel) of a shot of a snake, tongue flickering, coiling itself up a tree when Serge and Albine are in their personal 'Garden of Eden', Le Paradou, the huge

46 'summary aspect'.

wild garden belonging to the house in which Albine lives with her free-thinking guardian Jeanbernat, and the setting for the entire second part of Zola's three-part book.

Some of the most interesting changes Franju made to Zola's *La Faute de l'Abbé Mouret* relate to female characterisation and the representation of the feminine, and for this reason I shall discuss them in Chapter 4. The other notable criticism his film met with was, predictably, that it reduced an important literary work by politicising or 'ideologising' it: debate about whether celibacy in the priesthood was desirable had been active in France in the second half of the 1960s, and the centrality of this issue to Franju's film was unmissable – even though he had been wanting to make his adaptation since a time when it was not current and critical. Franju's own stated views on priests marrying were that he was 'plutôt partisan du mariage ... dans la mesure où je reste persuadé que cela entraînera la fin de tout mysticisme dans le catholicisme' (*Les Nouvelles littéraires* 15 October 1970).[47] Despite respecting the historical setting of Zola's *La Faute*, Franju's film also alluded to the saying of Mass in French rather than Latin (a novelty of 1965) and to the issue of 'prêtre-ouvriers',[48] another contemporary and therefore 'anachronistic' question the film's critics fell upon (*Combat* 13 October 1970; *Télérama* 1 November 1970).

Perhaps the most important issue raised by Franju's *La Faute*, however, is whether Zola's novel – despite lengthy descriptions of the impoverished rural setting of Les Artaud and a long central section composed principally of lyrical listings of trees, plants and flowers (particularly roses) – is actually a 'naturalist' novel at all, in the mode Zola theorised and in which he composed many of the novels in the Rougon-Macquart series. Franju stated that what he was studying in Serge Mouret's conflict between his love for Albine and his priestly calling was 'la grande lutte de la nature et de la religion' (*Le Figaro littéraire* 19 October 1970).[49] But he was convinced that although Zola may have been aspiring to naturalism in *La Faute de l'Abbé Mouret*, he had in fact exceeded naturalism and arrived at 'l'imaginaire, le fantastique' (*Le Figaro littéraire* 19 October 1970).[50] Claude Mauriac,

47 'more in favour of priests marrying than not ... in so far as I am convinced that it would bring an end to all the mysticism in Catholicism'.
48 'worker priests'.
49 'the great struggle between nature and religion'.
50 'an imaginary, fantastic world'.

reviewing in *Le Figaro littéraire*, agreed with him, seeing something quite distinct from realism (an 'irréalisme') in Zola's novel and confirming that Zola had transformed reality where he thought he was simply reproducing it. And Zola's avowed use of dictionaries and plant encyclopedias to find the myriad of names that make up his catalogued Garden of Eden reinforces this view: the central section of his novel is extremely languorous in terms of narrative, a linguistic performance rather than a representational one. Of course, identifying a non-realist linguistic excess in Zola's writing does not equate to recognising that Franju captured this non-naturalist imbalance of form and content in the *mise-en-scène* of his adaptation, and while I fully agree that Franju's film does not seem particularly interested in the plenitude of naturalistic visual representation, traces of the 'fantastique' (as atmosphere and distinct from fantasy as psychological projection, on which I shall comment in Chapter 4) are hard to detect. But Franju's reading of Zola was undoubtedly a subtle one not limited to ideological exploitation of a novel whose subject he felt strongly about, and Claude Mauriac was right to reserve judgement on his film, saying that later generations might appreciate it more than 1970s reviewers had done.

Conclusion

A comment made by *Libération* critic Matthieu Lindon on the occasion of the rerelease of *Pleins feux sur l'assassin* in 1992 can serve as a summary of the complexity and interest of Franju's relationship to cinematic genre: 'Et peut-être, en effet, le talent de Franju vient-il de ce qu'il y a toujours un léger tremblement entre ses films et le genre auquel on voudrait les assimiler mais auquel ils ne correspondent jamais tout à fait' (*Libération* 6 October 1992).[51] Rather than conforming to known, recognised genres, and exemplifying what Derrida calls 'the law of genre', Franju's *longs métrages* all refuse an easy 'fit' within one coherent and self-identical generic type. They question cinematic genre(s) and generic identity from within by mixing up the characteristics of different types and styles of film, or by

51 'Perhaps Franju's talent does in fact stem from the fact that there is always a slight "trembling" between his films and the genre in which one would like to classify them, but to which they never completely correspond'.

appearing to belong predominantly to a single genre when they in fact participate in several. One of Franju's talents as a director was to use his film-making to reflect self-consciously – some would say too self-consciously – on the genre(s) he was working with at any given moment. To some this makes him too 'arty' or too intellectual a film-maker, despite passionate involvement with the popular genres of the serial, the thriller and horror. In sum, the corpus of feature films Franju contributed to French cinema of the years 1958 to 1974 ranges across horror, the thriller, *film noir*, melodrama, and the literary adaptation, and offers rich material with which to study the intersection of a broad gamut of film genres with an *auteur*'s style. Far from just being France's representative of *cinéma fantastique*, Franju engaged with genre cinema with the same critical awareness, flair and verve as his French contemporaries, the American-influenced directors of the *nouvelle vague*.

References

Austin, Guy (2001), 'Gender in the French fantasy film 1965–95', in Alex Hughes and James Williams (eds), *Gender and French Cinema*, Oxford and New York, Berg, pp. 157–69.

Beja, Morris (1976) *Film and Literature*, London and New York, Longman.

Bellour, Raymond and Lacassin, Francis (1961), 'Pleins feux sur ... Boileau-Narcejac', *Cinéma* 54 (March), 21–31.

Beylie, Claude (1978), 'Le Dernier Mélo de Franju', *L'Ecran* 75 (December), 19–30.

Beylie, Claude and Schapira, Catherine (1984), 'Méliès, Franju, via Feuillade', Entretien avec Georges Franju, *L'Avant-Scène cinéma* 325/6 (April), 2–11.

Brown, Robert (1983), 'Georges Franju: behind closed windows', *Sight and Sound* 52(4) (autumn), 266–71.

Brumagne, Marie-Madeleine (1977), *Georges Franju. Impressions et aveux*, l'Age d'Homme, Lausanne.

Brunette, Peter and Wills, David (1989), *Screen/Play: Derrida and Film Theory*, Princeton NJ, Princeton University Press.

Buache, Freddy (1962), 'A propos de Thérèse Desqueyroux: entretien avec Georges Franju', *Image et Son* 155 (October), 10–15.

Buache, Freddy (1996), *Georges Franju: poésie et vérité*, Paris, Cinémathèque française.

Buss, Robin (1994) *French Film Noir*, London and New York, Marion Boyars.

Carbonnier, Alain and Collombat, Boris (1986), 'Franju ou le fantastique au quotidien', *Cinéma* 369 (24–30 September), 8.

Chevassu, François (1961), 'Review of *Pleins feux sur l'assassin*', *Image et son* 142 (June), 41.

Cook, Pam (1985), *The Cinema Book*, London, British Film Institute.

Cousins, Russell (2001), 'A qui *La Faute*...? Re-subverting the subversive: Franju's reworking of Zola's Garden of Eden story', *Excavatio* 15, 3–4 and 63–73.

Daney, Serge (1986), 'L'Oeil était dans la tombe et regardait Franju', *Libération* 25 September.

Delahaye, Michel (1961), 'Rocoquille perlière', *Cahiers du cinéma* 119 (May), 61–2.

Derrida, Jacques (1980), 'The law of genre', in *Glyph* 7, Baltimore, The Johns Hopkins University Press, 202–29.

Durgnat, Raymond (1967), *Franju*, London, Studio Vista.

Durgnat, Raymond (1996), 'Paint it black: the family tree of the *Film Noir*', in Alain Silver and James Ursini (eds), *Film Noir Reader*, New York, Limelight Editions, pp. 37–51.

Fieschi, Jean-André and Labarthe, André S. (1963), 'Nouvel entretien avec Georges Franju', *Cahiers du cinéma* 149 (November), 1–17.

Forestier, François (1986), 'Le Guetteur de l'insolite', *L'Express*, 12 September.

Harvey, Sylvia (1978), 'Woman's place: the absent family of film noir', in E. Ann Kaplan (ed.), *Women In Film Noir*, London, British Film Institute, pp. 35–46.

Magny, Joël (1992), 'Pleins feux sur Franju', *Cahiers du cinéma* 460 (October), 46–50.

Marlore, M. and Beylie, C. (1963) 'Comment je "refais" le *Judex* de Feuillade', *Les Lettres françaises*, 18 July.

Milne, Tom (1975),'Georges Franju: the haunted void', *Sight and Sound* 44(2) (spring), 68–72.

Mulvey, Laura (1989), 'Notes on Sirk and melodrama', in *Visual and Other Pleasures*, London and Basingstoke, Macmillan. First published in *Movie* 25 (1977/8).

Piton, Jean-Pierre (1995), '50 noms-clés du cinéma fantastique d'hier à aujourd'hui', *CinémAction* 74, 162–74.

Place, Janey, and Peterson, Lowell (1996), 'Some visual motifs of Film Noir', in Alain Silver and James Ursini (eds), *Film Noir Reader*, New York, Limelight Editions, pp. 65–73.

Schlockoff, Alain (1979), 'Entretien avec Georges Franju', *L'Ecran fantastique* 11, 58–70. Schrader, Paul (1996), 'Notes on Film Noir', in Alain Silver and James Ursini (eds), *Film Noir Reader*, New York, Limelight Editions, 53–63. First published in *Film Comment* 8(1) (spring 1972).

Thirard, Paul-Louis (1975), 'Un exercice de miroirs', *Positif* 165 (January), 60–1.

Truffaut, François (1954), 'Une certaine tendance du cinéma français', *Cahiers du cinéma* 31 (January 1954), 15–29.

Viviani, Christian (1974), 'L'Homme sans visage', *Positif* 162 (October) 53–4.

Wells, Paul (2000) *The Horror Genre: From Beelzebub to Blair Witch*, London, Wallflower.

1 Bonhomie amid the slaughter in *Le Sang des bêtes*.

2 View onto the cour de la Victoire, *Hôtel des Invalides*

3 Maria Casarès as Lady Macbeth, *Le Théâtre national populaire*

4 Franju and Edith Scob on the set of *Les Yeux sans visage*

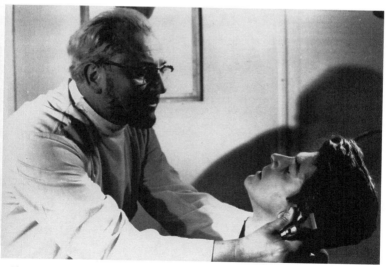

5 Threatening 'parental' authority (Dr Varmont and François) in *La Tête contre les murs*

6 Taking Edna Grüberg's body to the family tomb, *Les Yeux sans visage*

7 Married life (Thérèse and Bernard) in *Thérèse Desqueyroux*

8 Aborted kidnapping of Jacqueline, *Judex*

9 The devastation of the Great War, *Thomas l' Imposteur*

11 The man without a face, *Nuits rouges*

10 Serge Mouret turns his back on Albine, *La Faute de*

3

Mise-en-scène and the art of the real: Franju's cinematic aesthetics

As we have seen in the first two chapters of this study, Franju's cinema falls into two obvious parts, corresponding to the periods of his *courts* and *longs métrages* respectively. But although these periods are conveniently distinguishable, they are not in fact at all unified and distinct, either in themselves or from each other. When asked in 1962 what differences he saw between his short and feature films (at that point four in number), Franju replied 'A vrai dire, il n'y a pas grande différence' (Bureau 1962: 5).[1] More people were involved in feature-film-making, budgets were larger, and the work was easier since less discipline was required, but in moving from the short to the longer film he had neither felt nor intended any change of direction. *La Première Nuit* was a fictional and fantastic short, *La Tête contre les murs* as much an investigation into the reality of a psychiatric hospital as any documentary (Borde 1961: 10). In his shift into *long métrage* there was for Franju only continuity: stylistically and personally 'la façon de voir est la même' (Bureau 1962: 5).[2]

In the light of this continuity of style and approach I turn now to an exploration of the aesthetics of Franju's cinema, both *courts métrages* and feature films. The area of cinematic aesthetics – which can comprise at least the discussion of film images, their style, how the director may be placed in relation to the principal artistic movements of his age, and the personal responses of spectators to films – was much more dominant in film criticism during the years of Franju's activity as a director than it has usually been since. The major studies

1 'To tell the truth, there isn't much difference'.
2 'The way of seeing is the same'.

of Franju in French and English from the 1960s, by Vialle and Durgnat respectively, are in this mode, as is recent work in French by Gérard Leblanc. In devoting a chapter to Franju's aesthetics I shall largely be selecting from, summarising and combining the insights of these critics to construct a new synthesis of thinking about Franju's aesthetics, while adding my own responses to many scenes and moments in Franju's films. The main areas I shall take in – also privileged in existing studies because of their centrality – are Franju's use of décor and colour, his 'cinema of science', his use of framing and treatment of objects, and his relationship to realism and surrealism. A new area I shall be adding to this pantheon is Franju's filming of the human figure and face, which, unlike the other areas, has not been explored by any of the existing director-based studies.

A film-critical term of which I shall make particular use in this chapter, because it relates to all the aesthetic issues I have started to outline, is *mise-en-scène*. This can be defined as 'the contents of the frame and the way they are organised' (5). If the contents of the frame can quickly be enumerated as including at least décor, lighting, props, costumes and the actors themselves, then the organisation of these contents brings in the actors' relationships to each other, to the décor and to the camera (Gibbs 2002: 5).[3] *Mise-en-scène* is an apt term to employ when discussing Franju, since he can without too much controversy be allocated to the *mise-en-scène* side of the opposition film criticism has often constructed between *montage* and *mise-en-scène* cinema: while the former is organised rhythmically, characterised by fast cutting, and influenced by the figure and experimentation of Sergei Eisenstein, the latter is associated particularly with a number of great modernist directors Franju particularly admired, such as Fritz Lang and Jean Renoir. In his first influential article on Franju in 1955 Freddy Buache made the following central observation about Franju's proximity to the great directors of *mise-en-scène* cinema:

> Franju monte long, très long. Chez lui – contrairement à ce qui se passe chez un Rouquier, par exemple, fortement marqué par Eisenstein – ce n'est pas essentiellement de la succession des plans que naît

---

3 *Mise-en-scène* in the cinema is sometimes used as if in its (original) theatrical definition, but I agree with those critics who insist that it is used specifically of film images – a specificity constructed by the existence of a 'camera's-eye view' in relation to which all other elements of the scene are determined.

le rythme; c'est d'abord à l'intérieur même du plan que l'oeuvre prend son mouvement et, à ce propos, si je devais chercher quelque influence lointaine, c'est certainement chez les Nordiques – Sjöström notamment – que je me tournerais. (Buache 1955: 34)[4]

It is in early Swedish and German (as well as Europe-wide surrealist and 1930s French) cinema that the heirs to Franju's cinematic style are to be sought. Further support for the idea of Franju as a director of *mise-en-scène* comes from the fact that like other modernist French directors of the postwar period (Resnais, Marker, Robbe-Grillet), he is often referred to as a 'cinema poet'. Since *mise-en-scène* refers to visual style, all film criticism drawing on the terminology of 'film poetry' is in a sense associated with the idea and functioning of *mise-en-scène*.

Décor, contrast and colour

Turning now to analyses of the films themselves, my discussion begins with décor. In 1937 Franju revealed his awareness of the capacity of décor to produce meaning before narrative begins by writing that 'Le décor de Lang est un grand acteur' (Vialle 1968: 94).[5] There is limited scope for composed sets in Franju's documentaries, for obvious reasons, although *Le Grand Méliès* and *Monsieur et Madame Curie* constitute exceptions to the norm. While the sets of *Monsieur et Madame Curie* are memorable principally for an attitude to science I shall incorporate into my discussion of scientific cinema, the film's final shot makes particularly sentimental and nostalgic use of décor, by framing in a window onto a sunny exterior the flowers given by Pierre Curie to Marie just before his untimely death. Careful period detail is required for the overview of the life of Georges Méliès from the 1890s until 1937 given in *Le Grand Méliès*, and there are several scenes in which it is décor and props, rather than narrative action or commentary, that are crucial to the character and history being

4 'Franju's shots are long, very long. Unlike in Rouquier, for example, heavily influenced by Eisenstein, rhythm in Franju's films does not emerge from the way shots are joined together. It is from inside single shots that the work takes its movement, and if I had to identify some distant influence for this, it's to the Scandinavian directors – above all Sjöstrom – that I would turn.'

5 'Lang's sets are great actors'.

portrayed – the organised clutter of the toy stall Méliès kept at the Gare Montparnasse as an old man, and the paraphernalia of magic at shows given in his own Théâtre Robert Houdinot before his career in cinema began. In the opening drawing-room scene of the film gentle fade shots reveal the imprints of fresh cleanliness left by the removal of ornate upholstered furniture, and thus indicate the passing of time through the alteration of an interior. Décor and cinematography combine in the filmed reconstruction of a Méliès magic show, where a magician's-eye view through a transparent silk handkerchief Méliès is waving at his audience is followed by keyhole shots through the trick binoculars of a baffled female spectator. By using décor and props in this way Franju draws attention to seeing, concealing and revealing as the operations that enabled and inspired both Méliès' theatrical magic and his fantastic, illusion-based cinema. Another scene in *Le Grand Méliès* where cinematography self-reflexively enhances subject matter is the filming of the café Méliès enters in 1896 in search of Louis Lumière, having seen the poster advertising the Cinématographe Lumière on the boulevard outside. Franju shoots this as a shadow theatre of silhouettes through frosted glass, a further reminder of the nineteenth-century visual technologies drawn upon by early experimenters with the cinecamera.

In Franju's *longs métrages* the décor of interiors is, predictably, more important than in his documentaries. As I argued in Chapter 2, the creation of a sense of confinement is central to *La Tête contre les murs*, *Les Yeux sans visage*, and *Thérèse Desqueyroux*. The spacious, lavish and ornate interiors of châteaux are the main settings of both *Pleins feux sur l'assassin* and *Judex* (partly shot at the Musée Jacquemart André at Chaalis). These interiors support set pieces of great visual impact such as the masked ball where the banker Favraux 'dies'. As well as the galleries, courtyards, towers and secret rooms in *Pleins feux sur l'assassin*, which become spaces of paranoia because of the murder mystery plot (the loudspeakers of the sound system installed for the *son et lumière* resemble giant eyes), the castle's lakes and its open expanses of land used for riding convey an atmosphere of cold magnificence. A further link between this film and *Judex* is in the use of romantic ruins – the ruined castle and its underground vaults by the sea that is Judex's hideout and Favraux's prison, and the Carnac standing stones that form the setting of the semi-comic funeral scene that closes *Pleins feux sur l'assassin*. These romantic settings and décors create an aesthetic that can justifiably be described as gothic, and which is instrumental in constructing the genre(s) of the films concerned, as décor and *mise-en-scène* usually are.

In Franju's three adaptations of novels, décor is also often instrumental in creating atmosphere: Franju films the rooms of Bernard Desqueyroux's house as austere and even drab, in keeping with the stolid unimaginativeness of his character. However, décor is perhaps less important than other aspects of *mise-en-scène* and cinematography, in particular the use made of black and white and of colour respectively. Before the start of the interior monologue in which Thérèse narrates her story up to her return from trial, the white road stretching ahead of the car in pitch blackness figures the symbolic path of memories she has to negotiate. Most striking of all in this exploitation of contrast is the earliest scene in flashback, to before Thérèse's marriage, when Anne de La Trave arrives to meet her on a bicycle in glowing spring sunshine, dressed entirely in white. Thérèse herself is also dressed in white as she gets a ride on the back of Anne's cycle, and the scene powerfully conveys the joyful anticipation she is feeling at that point about her future marriage. Franju constructs this scene in deliberate contrast to an exterior the following spring, shortly after Thérèse has given birth to her daughter, when it is equally light and bright, but Thérèse is dressed entirely in black, detached from the rest of the world and hardly able to bear life at St-Clair any longer.

If the properties of black and white are deployed meaningfully in *Thérèse Desqueyroux*, this experimentation with light and its effects is extended in *Thomas l'imposteur* three years later. Here the story's Great War setting offers considerable scope for the filming of fire and explosions, a 'powerful vision of the destructiveness of war' (Armes 1985: 206), represented most memorably for many of the film's first spectators by the shot of a white horse with its mane on fire galloping through smoking ruins. Franju is more interested in such moments of pure contrast than in realistic depiction of fires of destruction or the artificial light in blacked-out trenches. In an early two shot of the Princesse de Bormes and Thomas in a Red Cross convoy vehicle, the repeated flashes of exploding cannon fire on the horizon behind them are the only movement, and in the abandoned farm where the princess's ambulance convoy is first allowed to tend the wounded (uselessly, since too many are already dying), a flickering fire creates dramatic contrasts of brightness and shadow. In the final sequence of the film firebombs and grenades explode in a black sky as Thomas makes the risky detour through trenches where he meets his death. Although all instances of fire and light are accounted for by the film's diegesis, the effects of Franju's deployment of light and lighting are in excess of this, and generate an atmosphere of unreality detached from destruction and suffering – a visual equivalent of the verbally playful and 'fantastic' qualities of Cocteau's writing.

Only four of Franju's films were shot in colour: the documentaries *Notre Dame, cathédrale de Paris* and *Sur le pont d'Avignon*, and his last two features. In each case colour is of considerable importance: in *Notre Dame* the dull but warm shades of the interior of the cathedral contrast with the grey, black and white of its exterior and of the winter landscape of Paris. The most striking shot in the film, the appearance above the nave of apparently suspended revolving red discs that turn out to be cardinals' hats, depends on colour as well as shape for its effect. In *La Faute de l'Abbé Mouret*, Franju's symbolic use of colour is distinct from the naturalism associated with Zola's novels, and not an attempt to imitate it. Colours of flowers and of Albine's dresses – salmon pink, orange, and shades of red and yellow – dominate the series of seven shots of the 'Garden of Eden' where Serge Mouret and Albine finally consummate their love. When the frail Mouret is assailed by the sin of his love for Albine in the form of visions, the church he is in turns into a deep red, flickering Hell. Overall, colour is instrumental to Franju's interpretation of the thematics of Zola's novel. In *Nuits rouges* the red of the man-without-a-face's mask is used for its traditional connotations of danger, as it distinguishes him from his underlings, and is also the colour that neutralises the advance of the army of mannequin robots. Shot in televisual Eastman color, *Nuits rouges* also depends heavily on this for the drama of its pulp plot of secret sects and ceremonies, and the allure of the evil heroine played by Gayle Hunnicutt.

Faciality and the human figure

In his introduction to a collection of papers given under the aegis of the *Collège d'histoire de l'art cinématographique* in 1994–95 and devoted to cinema's relationship to the human figure, Jacques Aumont sets out how the moving image, which had been invented as a technology of recording human movement, quickly discovered its anthropological capability. Early cinema defined itself as 'what makes man visible' (Aumont 1995: 7). The human figure revealed by the new technology and art of representation was 'l'homme classique', Cartesian man, understood as made up of a gesturing body and a face whose expressive powers were a window onto the soul. Silent cinema's discovery and development of the close-up privileged 'visagéité' or faciality. At the same time as it developed as a medium oriented around the representation of the human figure, however, cinema gave birth to a new idea of the *homo cinematographicus*, or specifically cinematic humanity: film did not just reveal an existing conception of humanity it inherited from other means of representation, it constructed a new one. An apparatus as well as an eye, film invented and constructed, through framing and montage, new figures of bodies, new ideals of corporeality (Aumont 1995: 7–8).

The human figure and face are a consistent focus of Franju's cinema, from his earliest short *Le Métro* through to the panoply of simulacra of bodies in *Nuits rouges*. In this section of the chapter I shall explore recurrent features in Franju's *homo cinematographicus*: his tendency to frame the head and face separately from the body; his interest in the topos of facelessness and the mask; his extensive use of isolating shots and close-ups of faces, and his 'facialising' of animals and non-human entities. In cinema as in photography, the face is almost always a signifier of humanity: 'support visible de la fonction la plus ontologique, le visage est *de l'homme*. Peu étonnant que l'humanisme sous toutes ses formes l'ait toujours exalté' (Aumont 1992: 14).[6] To facialise the non-human is to humanise, whereas to erase the face's expressive powers by masking them or blanking them out dehumanises: one has only to think of the eerie robot-like quality of zombies, cybermen or cinema's original invisible man in James Whale's 1933 film. If the quest for the *homo cinematographicus* has always been an analogical quest – how to represent people ('man') so that they most resemble ideal humanity – then along the way it has discovered the rich possibilities of representation of the *in*human. 'Entre défiguration et dissemblance ... il y fut question de ce qu'il advient de la figure humaine lorsqu'elle est attaquée, confrontée à ce qui l'excède ou lui est radicalement étranger ... L'homme du cinéma –

6 'the face, the visible support of the most ontological of functions, is *human*. Hardly surprising that all forms of humanism have always exalted it'.

... est aussi, ce n'est pas le moindre des paradoxes, le lieu de l'inhumain' (Aumont 1995: 8).[7]

Franju's fascination with the human figure is evident even when its representation is not being questioned, distorted, or played with. His repeated use of certain actors – Edith Scob, Emmanuelle Riva, Pierre Brasseur – is revelatory in this respect, as is the role of costume in creating suggestive auras for them that harmonise with the gothic or fantastical settings in which the action is located. Scob, who appears in four of Franju's first five films, has been called his *actrice-fétiche* (he did indeed superstitiously suggest that the lack of commercial success of *Pleins feux sur l'assassin* could be put down to failing to engage her for it (Vialle 1968: 36)). The mournful, desperate movements and gestures of Christiane in *Les Yeux sans visage* best exploit Scob's delicate, ethereal and haunting beauty, where her full, embroidered cape-like gowns (as well as her mask) lend her the doll-like rigidity that has so often been commented on. Her fragility is just as effective in her victimised, veiled Jacqueline Favraux in *Judex*, and in the pluckier yet naïve Anne in *Thérèse Desqueyroux*. To Franju, Riva was ideally cast as Thérèse in the latter film ('Et puis je connaissais Thérèse. C'était Emmanuèle Riva. Elle était l'image de la Thérèse écrite'[8] (Brumagne 1977: 49)) although her elegant and dignified beauty arguably make her more effective as the Princesse de Bormes in *Thomas l'imposteur*. There is a kind of fetishism in Franju's attachment to these two female stars that is actually most developed in relation to Francine Bergé and Syvia Koscina in *Judex*, playing the conspiring Diana Monti and Daisy the acrobat respectively. Usually clad in a black catsuit, Bergé is lovingly dwelt upon by the camera, with her sly, velvety movements and deft use of a knife usually held at her thigh and a hypodermic syringe with which she drugs Jacqueline before kidnapping her. As the catsuited accomplice of the man-without-a-face in *Nuits rouges*, Gayle Hunnicutt plays a similar role, and is filmed moving stealthily across rooftops and extracting poisoned blow-darts from her catsuit, which she aims expertly at her targets.

---

7 'Between disfigurement and dis-semblance ... the question was what happens to the human figure when it is attacked or confronted by what exceeds or is radically foreign to it ... It's a great paradox, but cinematic man – ... is also the site of the inhuman'.

8 'I already knew Thérèse. It was Emmanuelle Riva. She was the image of Thérèse in the book'.

Returning to *Judex*, the focus on Bergé's body is most memorable in two scenes of considerable athleticism: when she strips down to her catsuit from her disguise of a nun's habit to jump into the mill race and evade capture by Judex (shots up her body from below the trap door emphasise her lithe femininity), and when she and Daisy fight it out on the rooftop in the final scene. For this, Daisy's equally close-fitting circus athlete's garb is white, producing an obvious but striking symbolism of the struggle between the forces of good and evil.

Overall, of all Franju's films *Judex* is probably the richest in examples of the fetishised body, due in large part to the costumes inherited from Feuillade's serial. As the eponymous caped crusader, Channing Pollock cuts an imposing figure; less dashing and more solid is the physical authority of Pierre Brasseur as doctor in *La Tête contre les murs* and *Les Yeux sans visage*, and as aged patriarch at the start of *Pleins feux sur l'assassin*. When viewed from the perspective of body-fetishism, the trope of the missing body common to *Les Yeux sans visage*, *Pleins feux sur l'assassin* and *Judex* (in all three a character is missing supposed dead, although only in *Pleins feux* is this actually the case) takes on added significance, highlighting how the absence of the body propels narrative. Links between the *fantastique*, décor and atmosphere underpin most of Franju's cinema, as already discussed, and this applies to bodily appearance as much as to other elements of *mise-en-scène*. The inanimate figures that people *Nuits rouges* in the shape of zombies and *Hôtel des Invalides* as suits of armour are animated by their science-fiction status in the case of the first film, and by the speed with which the camera pans and whips from one to the next in the second. The position and use of the camera also breathes life into inanimate figures in *Notre Dame, cathédrale de Paris*, in medium shots of the gargoyles, and in *La Faute de l'Abbé Mouret* when Serge Mouret unpacks the new statue of the Virgin he has purchased for his church. Uncovering her doll-like face first, he then raises her up to a vertical position and to a height the angle of the shot makes appear equal to his own, although the statue is only two or three feet tall.

The first kind of construction I shall discuss in which Franju problematises the representation of the human figure is the detachment of head from body that can produce surreal, eerie or comic effects. One of the unusually long takes in *Le Métro* is of headless figures descending into the dark recesses of the underground from bright daylight outside, the camera positioned to sever the figures at the neck as they descend into view, identifying the Métro's users as one of modernity's faceless masses. Much more common in Franju's own films is the framing of the head without the body, and one way in which this is achieved is by emphasising the mask or headgear worn. Apart from *La Première Nuit*, where nuns appear in a few frames apparently solely for the visual pleasure afforded by the shape of their wimples, the masking of the human head and face is central to *Les Poussières*, *Les Yeux sans visage*, *Judex* and *Nuits rouges*. The large filter fitted over the lower face of a mechanically breathing experimental wooden head in *Les Poussières* gives it an elephantine distortion, while lights behind its eye-holes turn it into an animated horror movie humanoid. Industrial clothing worn by workers using sandblasting equipment turns them into cybermen; Franju's filming of these figures is unmistakably in excess of any straightforward documentary purpose. A similar surreal(ist) construction of the human figure occurs early in *Judex* when the eponymous hero arrives at the banker Favraux's castle to kidnap him, wearing an enormous bird-mask. As Franju points out, the image of Judex on the castle steps is pure 'insolite' or dislocation from context; Judex is unidentified to the spectator at this point, and it is only when he enters the castle that it becomes clear that he is attending a masked ball and the effect is attenuated (Brumagne 1977: 16) – although the scene is still perhaps Franju's purest example of the *fantastique*. In *Les Yeux sans visage*, facelessness is imposed on Christiane by both her disfigurement and her mask, and on Edna Grüberg by the bandages that swathe her head when her face has been surgically removed. 'Eyes without a face' describes Christiane, of course, but also the alarming close-up on Edna's bandaged face and staring eyes after she has jumped from an upstairs window, and the shots of Genessier's and his assistant's faces as they operate on their victims, hidden by surgical masks with only their eyes visible. In all these instances facelessness signifies inhumanity, either imposed and innocently suffered or consciously assumed. Eyes retain their traditional meaning of a 'window' onto the soul; her undamaged eyes glimmering through her mask are a major contributor to the pathos of Christiane's character.

The similarity of Franju's treatment of the human figure to Méliès's fantasy cinema is signalled in *Le Grand Méliès*, which includes an extract from a film called *The Man with the Rubber Head*, one of

Méliès' early experiments in trick photography from 1901. Using a black background, a dolly and double takes, Méliès creates a scene in which he appears to be blowing up his own head to an enormous size. Separation of the head from the body occurs again in *The Music Lover*, where the solid elements in the notes on a musical stave are each made of the tiny human head of a performer tossed up to the top of the stave, with multiple takes per frame allowing his head to reappear each time. As if to acknowledge Méliès' influence in fantastic constructions of the body, *Le Grand Méliès* shows him performing magic to two young boys at his Gare Montparnasse toyshop that involves the illusion of turning his head into a blossoming bouquet of flowers. Faced with a flower-headed eccentric, the two boys back away cautiously.

However, if Franju's privileging of the unattached head as body-part can be a source of humour and playfully filmed, this is not the prevailing mood when it comes to close-ups of the face, which is usually shown anxious, fearful or in distress. When Emmanuelle Riva's face is framed peering through tall grass in *Thérèse Desqueyroux*, it suggests her isolation, and when Maria Casarès is shot in close-up during her performance as Lady Macbeth in *Le Théâtre national populaire*, she is fully engaged in the character's tortured anguish and guilt. Highly *cinéma-vérité*-style close-ups on the village children's faces in *La Faute de l'Abbé Mouret* convey their poverty and illiteracy. Franju's fascination with the face and his aesthetic of cruelty – the refusal to stop short of the depiction of killing, maiming, disfigurement and deformity – come together most clearly in *Hôtel des Invalides* and *Les Yeux sans visage*, in shots of the war veterans and of Christiane Genessier. In the scene in the *Invalides* chapel, the camera lingers on a particularly disfigured man head-on for an uncomfortably long time, causing the spectator's gaze to recoil. Another powerful image of disfigurement is supplied to Franju by the museum's collection in the bronze head of Général Mangin, inexplicably gashed from the chin to the back of the neck, so that a whole portion of the bust is missing, and the head sits at a tilt. The camera executes a fascinated 180-degree pan round this exhibit, to the accompaniment of a jaunty Maurice Jarre polka.

The plot of *Les Yeux sans visage*, like a number of horror and science-fiction films before and since, is entirely woven around the idea that to be faceless is to be without a social identity, unviewable by and unacceptable to the world. Eugen Shuftan's photography of Franju's imagery of faces, masks and facelessness haunts more powerfully than any drama of looks, perhaps simply because of the subliminal hold that facial form has on spectatorial perception. The film's central scene of surgery – the operation on Edna Grüberg – is its most graphic illustration of the paradoxical significance of the face: the spectator is taken right through it in a sequence which lasts more than six minutes and culminates in the lifting away of the mask-like slice of skin that is Edna's face, to reveal a monstrous mass of bloody tissue beneath. There is no doubt here that we are in the realm of the inhuman, 'disfigurement' at its most literal and most extreme, more horrible than any elaborately constructed science fiction alien. The last shot of the sequence is a perfect illustration of the most striking quality of the face in the film, which is to be detachable and transferable, a graft – the 'heterograft' (*hétérogreffe*), about which Genessier lectures to an admiring audience in an earlier scene. The notion of the graft, like the Derridean supplement, undoes the logic of totality and completion; something which is part of one entity is attached to another as the condition of the 'foreign body's' survival. A surgical graft can be taken from the patient's own body in the case of skin, but in the case of organs always comes from a different body. The detachment of the graft from its host body in *Les Yeux sans visage* means, effectively, the death of that body, which has been rendered inhuman by the surgery. The face therefore has the potential (it fails to do this in the film) to act as the graft of humanity, the human graft.

Two further examples of the 'facialisation' of the non-human in Franju's cinema add to my claim about the importance of constructions of the face to his films. The first is a set of shots of Genessier's dogs that occurs at the end of *Les Yeux sans visage*, just before Christiane lets them loose and they maul him (the punishment for his cruel science is to be left with a bloody, ruined face). Here, the camera moves from dog to dog with swift but compassionate close-ups, focusing on the animals' eyes and features in a manner that humanises them by photographically constructing faces. These shots correspond extremely closely to a series at the end of *Mon chien*, where the abandoned dogs in their cages are filmed one by one, as the commentary informs us they will be taken to be gassed if not claimed. Although *Mon chien* is the single film of Franju's that tips over into sentimentality, the facialising and humanising of the dogs at this point works in effective counterpoint to the bleak commentary, so that the parallel of the 'humane' disposal of abandoned dogs with extermination in concentration camps is perturbing and thought-provoking rather than sentimental. The second example occurs in *Notre Dame, cathédrale de Paris* when, after a tracking shot up the nave of the cathedral, the camera rises and turns to take in the altar table and twin pillars, framing them into what is unmistakably the shape of a face. It is interesting to note that these facialisations in *Mon chien* and *Notre Dame, cathédrale de Paris* occur in two *courts métrages* that are otherwise almost devoid of actors, and therefore of the human figure.

Franju's constructions of the face can therefore be seen to range across the entire gamut of possibilities it offers to the cinematic image, from documentary pathos to the mesmerising 'dissemblance' of the human to itself in *Les Yeux sans visage*. Facialisation as a photographic and framing device reveals a further dimension of Franju's deployment of the face and its appurtenances, one that goes beyond its role as a signifier of the human. This is an interest in its geometry, its contours given abstract form, for obvious reasons usually the form of a circle. So the surreal red cardinals' hats of *Notre Dame, cathédrale de Paris* that metonymically represent ecclesiastical authority appear as rotating discs, the porcelain worker of *Les Poussières* holds up his plate so that it takes the place of his face, and Georges Méliès performs magic that replaces his head with a perfectly spherical bouquet of flowers.

Franju's cinema of science

Franju's 'favourite' film united the aesthetic qualities he valued most highly, which were horror, poetry and plasticity.[9] *Trépanation pour crise d'épilepsie Bravais-Jacksonnienne* was a scientific film about surgical technique by surgeon Thierry de Martel shot as the Second World

9 'Bien souvent on m'a demandé quel était, selon mes attirances personnelles et non par les influences que j'en avais reçues, le film le plus poétique du cinéma et je citais Buñuel, le plus beau film d'épouvante, et je citais Murnau, le film le plus plastique, et je citais Lang' (I've often been asked what cinema's most poetic film was, and I said Buñuel, the most beautiful horror film, and I said Murnau, the most plastic film, and I said Lang. This is according to personal taste, not to the influence the films had on me) (Franju, quoted in Vialle 1967: 86).

War was getting underway in 1940, though not shown until 1946. To Franju, it was a horror film of the highest order, poetic, extraordinarily 'plastic', effectively realist and yet unquestionably surrealist. Franju's interest in and esteem for the cinema of science was a constant from early in his career, and in 1945 he took over the direction of France's Institut de Cinématographie Scientifique from Jean Painlevé, a position he held until 1953. In this section I shall look at how science is treated in Franju's cinema, and how its significant place in his oeuvre is related to his cinematic aesthetics. The first part will be an exposition of French scientific cinema up to the 1950s, the period when Franju engaged with it; and the second, a commentary on the four of his films (three documentaries and *Les Yeux sans visage*) in which science figures significantly, and their different approaches to it.

Science, scientists and scientific experiment figure as object and image of the cinecamera from the days of film's inventors, and France is no exception. The recognised pioneer of scientific cinema in France, assisted early on by Charles Pathé and maker of over a hundred *courts métrages* between 1908 and 1970, was a Dr Jean Comandon, whose films of the interior of the human body were reviewed in the press of the 1910s and 1920s with the lyrical enthusiasm reserved for the avant-garde cinema of the time (Gauthier 1995: 50). This tendency of the scientific film to attract attention more for its aesthetic interest than for its content is a constant in the cinema of science in France up to and beyond Franju. Comandon is credited with the invention of 'micro-cinématographie', on which he published a book in 1943 (Porcile 1965: 258), and his output included both research films on surgery and radiography and commercially released documentaries such as *Le Scorpion* (1911) and *Champignons prédateurs* (1945).

Little known and rarely viewed corners of the work of Georges Méliès touch on scientific subject matter, but the film-maker who towers above all others in this field is Jean Painlevé, a friend of Artaud, Vigo and Eisenstein, and a founder member of the surrealist movement. Painlevé trained as a biologist before becoming diverted into film, and most of his over 200 documentaries are about underwater life, including the acclaimed *L'Hippocampe* of 1934. He was also a tireless protester and organiser, was active in pioneering underwater exploration, and founded the Institut de Cinématographie Scientifique, the world's first Institute for Scientific Cinema. Painlevé, who according to André Bazin 'occupe dans le cinéma français une place singulière et privilégiée'[10] (Bazin 1983: 222), is most acclaimed for a kind of poetry of the bizarre, the fantastic or the humorous often achieved through the combination of closely observed images, didactic explicative commentaries and upbeat jazz soundtracks that suspend or at least challenge the then relatively 'safe' dichotomy between science and art. Painleve's 'signature' films in this regard are *Assassins d'eau douce* of 1947, the musical accompaniment to which is Duke Ellington's 'Stompy Jones' and 'White Heat', and *Le Vampire* of 1945. This account of the life and habits of the South American vampire bat both returns to the origins of the myth of vampirism in the natural world and pays explicit homage to a founding cinematic representation of that myth, F.W. Murnau's *Nosferatu* of 1922.

The two other French directors of scientific cinema who must be included in any sketch of its history in the first half of the twentieth century are Jean-Benoit Lévy, active in the 1920s and 1930s, and Pierre Thévenard, author of *Le Cinéma scientifique français* (1948) (one of the few books on scientific cinema to be published in this period) and directing from 1934 into the 1960s. Lévy, apart from being Secretary of the Comité français d'études médico-chirurgicales par le cinématographe, whose mission statement outlined its aims of progress in biological (and especially surgical) research and teaching through the application of cinema as a technology (Porcile 1965: 232), made some of the earliest surgical films alongside those of Comandon, films on particular medical techniques such as *La Bronchoscopie* (1932) and *Cancer du sein* (1933), and eventually pioneered the technique of endoscopy to achieve tracking shots inside the human body. Thévenard, meanwhile, was in charge of the film laboratory of the Institut Pasteur from 1943 onward, and was the maker of acclaimed documentary shorts on insects and animals (*Les Aventures d'une mouche bleue* (1958) and *La Giraffe à Paris* (1959)) as well as the director of numerous medical and surgical films.

French scientific cinema's most noted spokesman amongst critics and theorists of its first six decades was undoubtedly André Bazin, who enthused about the genre while declining to define it as either a subclass or category apart of the documentary. For Bazin, this type of cinema might seem to be situated on the scientific side of the art–science divide because of having its origins in technical experimentation, but

10 'occupies a singular and privileged position in French cinema'.

was most definitely to be claimed for art, and (one is tempted to add) for the apogee of Bazinian realism:

> Lorsque Muybridge ou Marey réalisaient les premiers films d'investigation scientifique, ils n'inventaient pas seulement la technique du cinéma, ils créaient du même coup le plus pur de son esthétique. Car c'est là le miracle du film scientifique, son inépuisable paradoxe. C'est à l'extreme pointe de la recherche intéressée, utilitaire, dans la proscription la plus absolue des intentions esthétiques comme telles, que la beauté cinématographique se développe par surcroît comme une grâce surnaturelle. (Bazin 1983: 221)[11]

Implicitly paying homage to Lévy and explicitly to Painlevé, Bazin suggests that scientific cinema was responsible for pushing back the boundaries of images acceptable to its age. It purveyed hard truths, an unbearable realism ('Il n'est malheureusement pas certain que cette éblouissante vérité puisse être communément supportée'[12] (Bazin 1983: 222)). Bazin goes so far as to estimate the surgical cinema of Thierry de Martel 'beyond' surrealism:

> Mais Tanguy, Salvador Dali ou Buñuel n'ont jamais approché que de loin ce drame surréaliste, où le regretté docteur de Martel, pour pratiquer une trépanation compliquée, sculpte au préalable sur une nuque rasée et nue comme une coquille d'oeuf l'esquisse d'un visage. Qui n'a pas vu cela ignore jusqu'où peut aller le cinéma. (Bazin 1983: 221)[13]

I shall return to Bazin's estimation of surgical cinema and make a counter-suggestion to Bazin about Franju's aesthetics after looking at the four films of Franju's that explicitly feature science, scientists and/or scientific photography. They represent four distinct types of 'scientific' film. The first, *Monsieur et Madame Curie*, falls into the sub-genre of 'homages to great scientists', following the silent *Pasteur*

---

11 'When Muybridge and Marey made the first investigative scientific films, they were not just inventing cinematic technique, they were creating, simultaneously, film's purest aesthetic. For this is the miracle, the inexhaustible paradox of scientific cinema: it is at the extreme of goal-oriented, utilitarian research, when aesthetic intentions as such have been absolutely ruled out, that cinematic beauty develops, excessively, like supernatural grace'.

12 'Unfortunately it isn't certain that this dazzling truth is generally bearable'.

13 'But Tanguy, Salvador Dali or Buñuel never got near the surrealist drama in which the late-lamented Dr Martel prepares for surgery by sculpting the sketch of a face onto a neck that is shaven and naked as an eggshell. Anyone who hasn't seen this is unaware of how far cinema can go.'

made by Jean Epstein and Jean-Benoit Lévy in 1922. The second, *Les Poussières*, is an industrial scientific documentary, much in the mode of Godard's first seventeen-minute film of the same year, *Opération béton*. *A propos d'une rivière*, as set out in Chapter 1, is a documentary set in a fictional framework, a style of *court métrage* Franju would tend towards increasingly throughout the 1950s. The fourth of Franju's scientific films is that peculiarly medical *film fantastique* that is *Les Yeux sans visage*.

It is tempting to see *Monsieur et Madame Curie* as the product of a competitive French or European backlash to the flurry of films about the lives of great scientists that came out of Hollywood in the 1940s. Mad scientists far outnumber sane and saintly ones in twentieth-century cinema, as Christopher Frayling observes (Frayling 2000: 18–19), but an interlude in the predominance of mad and erroneous science at this time saw the major Hollywood studios temporarily give way to a series of biopics such as Warner Bros' *The Story of Louis Pasteur*, Twentieth Century Fox's *The Story of Alexander Graham Bell*, and MGM's *Young Tom Edison* and *Edison the Man*, starring Mickey Rooney and Spencer Tracy respectively. In 1943 MGM made a large-budget dramatisation of Marie Curie's story called *Madame Curie*, starring Greer Garson.

Whereas the majority of American narrativisations of scientists' lives echo the conventions of mad-scientist films by showing their subjects 'treated as crazy by the establishment; ... sacrific[ing] domestic life to the interests of science, channelling their emotions into their work rather than their relationships' (Frayling 2000: 19), French homages to 'men of science' (generally men of course) are usually genuine homages, and patriotic if not nationalistic. In Franju's film of the Curies the first striking feature is the semiotic authority granted to scientific knowledge and apparatus through Franju's use of the camera. A slow zoom in on a question mark in the periodic table sets up the unknown chemical element being sought for the spectator; there are *plans fixes* on an electrometer and an ionisation chamber, and repeated shots of a bearded Pierre gravely demonstrating formulae and equations at the blackboard.

The second striking feature of *Monsieur et Madame Curie* is developed to a greater extent in *Les Poussières*, as it is only alluded to in the first short through a shot of a flame in the dark that metonymically stands in for the invisible energy of radioactivity. *Les Poussières* deals mainly with the industrial dust of mines and cement and porcelain factories, though also features atomic and astronomic dust: it opens with an iris out on a galaxy of stars (the dust floating free in the universe is equal in weight to all the heavenly bodies put together), and a series of shots of striking skies coloured by dust from the sun, of the desert, the sea's salt 'dust' and the pollen in Paris's parks. All these forms of dust are invisible, but the film's main aim is to record the often microscopic dust particles that destroy human tissue, in this case that of the lung. One point at which this paradoxical attempt at filming invisibility is indicated is in shots of a transparent plate of fine porcelain through which the factory worker views his shadowy hand; another is a shot of an X-ray photograph of silicosis in a worker's lung, indicated by arrows because the presence of the disease can only be interpreted by the expert eye. *Les Poussières* ends with a shot of an atomic explosion (the word 'FIN' appearing from out of the mush-room cloud) and at this moment, and in its implied critique of the industrial practices that cause disease in workers, articulates a critique of radioactivity and harmful science that the 'homage' genre of *Monsieur et Madame Curie* could not comfortably contain. The cinematography of *Les Poussières* also demonstrates the authority of scientific endeavour, in several shots of white-coated laboratory investigators using their equipment, and in shots of the scientific apparatus itself – a beaker of water into which industrial dust from an experimental filter is dissolved in order to analyse it, and a small inverted glass funnel around which dust is blown at high speed to measure its movement.

If *Les Poussières* is a critical counterpart to *Monsieur et Madame Curie*, its shots of the damaged body also anticipate key moments in *A propos d'une rivière* and *Les Yeux sans visage*. In Franju's 1950s work the development of what he called the 'aesthetic realism' of *Le Sang des bêtes* occurs mainly through his treatment of science and nature, and involves further representation of cruelty and disfigurement. As Freddy Buache notes of *A propos d'une rivière*, 'A l'intérieur d'un sport bonhomme, Franju dévoile un système de tuerie exactement pareil à celui des abattoirs' (Buache 1996: 41).[14] Cruelty is highlighted most pointedly in a sequence in which a huge salmon is hooked out of the

14 'At the heart of a good-natured sport, Franju uncovers a system of butchery exactly like that of the abattoirs'.

water after a tussle then finished off by being hit brutally on the head six times with a large stone. Photographically speaking, the most absorbing sequence of the film is in a kind of flashback inserted to explain the procedure for 'tagging' the salmon before it began its journey downstream. Shots of how the 'pièce d'identité' (a tiny letter rolled into a celluloid tube) is sewn into the 8cm-long baby fish directly anticipate Franju's filming of human surgery in *Les Yeux sans visage*. After irising out to laboratory-style filming in which the tagging is carried out, the camera's eye becomes microscopic (and also highly humanistic, with a shot of the tiny fish's heart beating), before irising in again on the baby fish back in the water. Microscopic filming or micro-cinematography also features several times in *Les Poussières*, where pulmonary infections and the destructive power of the deadly 'poussière de silice' on a squirming human blood cell are examined, and the Brownian motion of miniscule particles of dust demonstrated.

Les Yeux sans visage, Franju's only fiction film to explore scientific themes, has long been recognised as an early example of 'realist horror', a subcategory of horror that again became of particular interest with the advent of serial killer movies such as Jonathan Demme's *The Silence of the Lambs* and related real-life crimes and criminals (Freeland 1998). In realist horror the boundaries between fiction and fact are harder to discern; criminals and monsters cannot easily be kept at the safe aesthetic distance of fiction. The science of skin grafting and reparative plastic surgery on which the plot of *Les Yeux sans visage* is based was possible at the time the film was made, even if the full-scale face transplant Genessier aspires to for his disfigured daughter was not. Genessier himself is not a mad or evil scientist, but (as Franju was at pains to emphasise in interviews about the film (Borde 1961: 10)) a sane, guilty and desperate one. The horror of the film lies in his misplaced faith in science to make good human error.

Franju's filming of surgery and the grotesque results of its failure in *Les Yeux sans visage* shows him to be the direct heir in French cinema of Painlevé's blend of the scientific and the fantastic. Franju's one incursion into 'science fiction', anchored in reality and the everyday while also managing to be a prime example of the *fantastique*, is a predictable successor to the treatment of science to be found in his documentaries, both thematically and filmically. Just as Painlevé's narrativisation of the lives of sea creatures and the vampire bat through the addition of contrapuntally incongruous soundtracks reveals a blend of the imaginative and the investigative characteristics of the best documentary (fictional or narrative elements pertaining to animal life are not suppressed), Franju's exploration in a fictional framework of the images of cruelty that had fascinated him since at least 1948 demonstrates the artistic operation that turns disturbing or violent everyday images into horror and the bizarre.

I can now return to Bazin's claim that the investigative scientific cinema of Muybridge and Marey – and, by extension, that of French film-makers such as Painlevé and Franju – creates cinema's purest aesthetic. Bazinian realism turns this observation into an 'inépuisable paradoxe':[15] how can such finely crafted art emerge simply from filming materiality? But Bazin's paradox only becomes one by virtue of the binary opposition between documentary realism and magical fantasy on which his argument depends, itself a version of the opposition between the Lumières and Méliès familiar from early French cinema, when the short films of Auguste and Louis Lumière were (mistakenly) assumed to be naturalistic documentaries, and those of Méliès received as the products of pure fantasy. This opposition was always open to deconstruction, and has recently been thoroughly rethought by film criticism, which has pointed out the staged and fictional character of many of the Lumières' shorts. Franju's admiration for and sympathy with Méliès is clear, but his comment on the perceived opposition between Méliès and the Lumières is highly revealing, and itself implicitly deconstructive: 'J'adore Méliès, c'est le plus grand, mais il rêve à ma place. Alors que Lumière me fait rêver' (Chevrie 1986: 47).[16] Despite his preference for Méliès, it was the Lumières' approach to cinema that inspired Franju, because it opened onto the real, rather than substituting itself for his own vision. To Franju, 'reality' was inspiration enough, and there was nothing paradoxical about making aesthetically beautiful images from microscopic and surgical 'facts'. Seen from this perspective, his scientific cinema, like *Trépanation pour crise d'épilepsie Bravais-Jacksonnienne*, is a prime example of the art of the real.

15 'inexhaustible paradox'.
16 'I adore Méliès, he's the greatest, but he dreams for me. Whereas Lumière makes me dream'.

The art of the real

As my discussion of Franju's cinema of science has shown, cinematic documentation of the 'deep', composite nature of material reality is often understood to be realistic in essence. Varieties of realism pervade critical discussion of Franju's work, from the 'réalisme fantastique' inherited from his homages to Feuillade through to 'aesthetic realism', Franju's own term for the preoccupation with unseemly and violent acts and actions that marks his films from *Le Sang des bêtes* on. While 'réalisme fantastique' is oxymoronic, 'aesthetic realism' is rather tautologous: how can one director's sensory record of the world be anything other than 'aesthetic', do anything more than or different from expressing a response to the objects and forms he or she sees?[17] These difficulties of terminology are reinforced by Franju's tendency throughout his career to describe and justify his own work as 'realist'. The sense given to 'realist' in these instances is, however, often

17 Feuillade was the originator in French cinema of the mix of genres known as *réalisme fantastique*, a genre 'label' that recurs constantly in critical responses to Franju's cinema, and particularly *Judex*, for obvious reasons. Because Franju's *Judex* 'survenait en pleine période cinéphilique de réévaluation du passé' (came about in a cinephile era given over to reevaluating the past) (Buache 1996: 52), and is in narrative terms a faithful pastiche of Feuillade's film, it is understandable that it should have been received as Feuilladian *réalisme fantastique*. The best example of this view is Jacques Siclier's review for *Le Monde* (1987), in which Siclier coins the expression 'fantastique social' as a synonym for *réalisme fantastique*, and classifies all Franju's films up to *Judex* as belonging to this generic mix rather than any other. What appears at first to be a self-contradictory expression does make some sense in reference to Feuillade's combination of precise décors, charismatic characters, and racy story-lines packed with narrative peripetia: the mystery and power of Feuillade's world arises out of its representation of reality. But the expression *réalisme fantastique* also has a critical function rarely commented on (an exception is the chapter entitled 'Fantastic realism' in Ezra 2000), which is to attempt to reconcile the two very different styles of cinema pursued by the pioneers of its early years, the Lumière brothers and George Méliès. Since these styles were widely perceived as opposing documentary realism to magical fantasy, a cinema which combined them was highly desirable at a time when national cinemas were in the process of taking shape, cinematic genres more flexible than they were to become with the rise of Hollywood, and designations of genre less critically scrutinised. In this context it is also worth remembering that Feuillade was the artistic director of Gaumont, and that the New York branch of Pathé, still a French company at the time, was looking for subjects to compete with the huge audiences his serial films were drawing into cinemas (Durgnat 1967: 107).

almost zero: in conversation with Raymond Borde in 1961 he stated 'Je suis réaliste par la force des choses ... Cela me semble imposé par les conditions mêmes du spectacle cinématographique' (Borde 1961: 8).[18] All Franju is saying here is that the film image is, to use the language of the American semiotician Charles Peirce, an iconic sign. Franju's main motivation for calling himself a realist is not any particular interest in the process and perfectibility of mimesis, but his fascination with the real, whether investigated in documentary or in fiction. Despite his links to the *fantastique*, he had no interest in the excesses of fiction and the imagination usually associated with horror and science fiction cinema: 'Pierre Kast me demandait l'autre jour pourquoi je ne réalisais pas un sujet de science-fiction. Je lui ai répondu que j'aimais la science, mais pas la fiction' (9).[19] For Franju, horror and the *fantastique* arose not from the indulgence and free flight of the imagination, but directly from observation of the real, which could supply all the fear anyone might need. In a 1986 interview Franju agreed with Marc Chevrie that there is an ontological link between cinematic spectacle and fear, and that 'known' reality is far more frightening than the unknown: cinema might be termed an 'ontological obscenity' (Chevrie 1986: 44). Lumière's *Arrivée d'un train dans la gare de Ciotat* was a horror film, because its spectators were sufficiently unfamiliar with the cinematic medium to believe that the train was going to plough through the auditorium; or, as Franju puts it, 'Je serais beaucoup plus effrayé par une poignée de porte que par les Martiens. Je me fous des Martiens, je ne les connais pas' (46).[20] Everyday reality supplies more than enough strangeness and horror for film narrative, and to create these atmospheres and effects, film-makers simply need to train their imagination(s) on the real, a process encapsulated in Boileau-Narcejac's epigraph to *La Première Nuit*: 'Il suffit d'un peu d'imagination pour que nos gestes les plus ordinaires se chargent soudain d'une signification inquiétante, pour que le décor de notre

18 'I am a realist by the nature of things ... It seems to me to be compelled by the very conditions of cinematic spectacle'.

19 'Pierre Kast asked me the other day why I didn't make a science-fiction film. I told him that I liked science, but not fiction'.

20 'I would be much more frightened by a door handle than by Martians. What do I care about Martians, I don't know them!'

vie quotidienne engendre un monde fantastique'.[21]

In the light of all these 'anti-realist' indicators, I shall argue in this final section of the chapter, against Franju and most of the criticism of his work produced during his lifetime, that despite his contribution to narrative cinema, it is not useful to describe him as a realist film-maker. Instead, I shall suggest that it is precisely Franju's questioning of realism(s) – the interrogation of the film spectator's relationship to the real to be found in both his *courts* and *longs métrages* – that is the most important element of his oeuvre, and the one that most clearly defines his cinematic style. The apparently realist mode of his *longs métrages* alternates constantly with 'surrealist' moments, shots and atmospheres, and these have to be accounted for. My comments on the other aspects of *mise-en-scène* mentioned at the start of this chapter, framing and the treatment of objects, will be incorporated into this discussion, which will give consideration to Franju's own rather obsessive explanations of his aesthetic procedures, to his relationship to the cinematic movements that preceded him (expressionism, surrealism and French poetic realism of the 1930s), and to his preference for the unexpected and for visual disjunctures (the 'insolite').

In the main director-based studies of Franju's work there is at least unanimity that his approach to representing the real is central to his film-making: as Vialle puts it, Franju's films are 'miroirs de l'insolite, perturbateurs de nos perceptions du réel' (Vialle 1968: 176).[22] Jean Cocteau observed of *Les Yeux sans visage* that Franju had not forgotten the important rule in horror cinema about treating the unreal with the maximum of realism (175), while Jean-Luc Godard's response to *La Tête contre les murs* was a more enthusiastic and nuanced discovery of the same combination of real and unreal: '*La Tête contre les murs* est un film *inspiré*. Pour Franju, aller jusqu'au bout des choses a consisté cette fois à surprendre non pas la folie derrière le réalisme, mais de nouveau le réalisme derrière cette folie elle-même' (174–5).[23] All these comments identify a characteristic oscillation in Franju's films between

21 'A little imagination is sufficient for our ordinary gestures suddenly to become charged with worrying meaning, for the décors of our everyday lives to engender a fantastic universe'.

22 'mirrors of the "insolite" that upset our perceptions of the real'.

23 '*La Tête contre les murs* is an *inspired* film. For Franju, this time, getting to the bottom of things has meant locating not just the madness behind realism, but the realism behind this madness itself'.

realism and its others, an instability that explains why spectators' and critics' responses to Franju's films so often refer to their quality of anxiety (*angoisse* or *inquiétude*). They present a recognisable world, but in a manner – or with a 'regard' – that perturbs our sense of the real, pulling it in unfamiliar directions. Despite often presenting himself as a realist, Franju's own views on representing 'reality' were very much in tune with the impression his films made – that poetry (with the terms 'poetry', 'non-realism' and 'surrealism' being inter-changeable in this instance) is amid or part of the real: 'Le rêve, la poésie, l'insolite doivent émerger de la réalité même. Tout le cinéma est documentaire, surtout le plus poétique' (Chevrie 1986: 46).[24] Or, in an alternative formulation that makes the link to surrealist cinema:

> Buñuel a dit un jour: 'Dans tous les films, bons ou mauvais, au-delà et malgré les intentions des réalisateurs, la poésie cinématographique lutte pour venir à la surface et se manifester.' Cela ne veut-il pas dire que la poésie est dans la réalité, dans la vie même des films, et qu'il s'agit moins de l'exprimer que de ne pas l'empêcher de se manifester? (Franju, quoted in Vialle 1968: 84)[25]

Realism is already surrealism; Franju avowed an adolescent fondness for Freud, for German psychology in general, and for its style of explor-ing mystery (Vialle 1968: 90). He was happy to declare his affinity with surrealism – 'Je suis en plein accord et depuis toujours avec les surréalistes. Ils m'ont beaucoup apporté' (Lebovits and Tranchant 1959: 20).[26]

But as both Durgnat and Vialle explain (the latter classes Franju roundly *as* a surrealist), what links Franju to the surrealist movement is not some vague embrace of its fashionableness or any interest in its claims to be revolutionary, but a singular development and manipu-lation of the aesthetic of the 'insolite' (Leblanc 1992: 16). In surrealist art, which abounds with monstrous forms, this is usually understood

24 'Dream, poetry, and the "insolite" must emerge from reality itself. All cinema is documentary, especially the most poetic'.

25 'Buñuel said one day: "In all films, good or bad, beyond and in spite of directors' intentions, cinematographic poetry is struggling to come to the surface and reveal itself". Doesn't this mean that poetry is in reality, in the very life of films, and that it is less a question of expressing it than of preventing it from revealing itself?'

26 'I have always been in full agreement with the Surrealists. I have learned a great deal from them' (Franju, quoted in Durgnat 1967: 18).

as an aesthetic of the bizarre and the monstrous. Franju's interest in such forms is evident, but his deployment and treatment of them is far subtler. The 'insolite' in Franju, as Leblanc states, is an eruption of the discontinuous in familiar continuity – Christiane's decaying face graft photographed after an everyday if newly hopeful family supper in *Les Yeux sans visage* – a dislodging of the everyday which mobilises the viewer's imagination and sensibility (62). The technique on which it depends is one of juxtaposition with poetic force (Franju, quoted in Vialle 1968: 95), a juxtaposition which is usually a disjuncture. Franju goes so far as to make this disjuncture of context the *raison d'être* of two of his documentaries:

> Si l'Hôtel des Invalides n'était pas situé dans Paris, si la Seine n'y coulait pas à côté, je n'aurais pas filmé l'*Hôtel des Invalides*. Si les aciéries de Lorraine n'étaient pas entourées de champs de blé, je n'aurais pas tourné *En passant par la Lorraine*. (Lebovits and Tranchant 1959: 23)[27]

What distinguishes Franju's striking juxtapositions of objects and scenes from many better remembered surrealist ones, the classic example being the slicing of a human eye with a razor in Buñuel's *Un chien andalou*, is that they are not designed to shock the viewer or to convey an association with a meaning personal to the director, or with any established meaning. Instead, they jolt our perception, sharpen our vision of reality. As Durgnat puts it, 'the reference is not just to someone's psyche, but to a world in which we might all move. In Franju, the reference is constantly to the objective world in which we do all move, and at which our eyes unseeingly stare. Far from cutting out the real world, his vision lets it in' (Durgnat 1967: 19).

Some of the best examples of Franju's technique of disjuncture occur early in *Le Sang des bêtes*, in shots of a man seated at a table on a piece of waste ground near the abattoirs of la Villette, and of a lovers' kiss. In the shot of the round dining table, not only is its presence on this wasteland unexplained, but a double disjuncture is created by the attitude of the man seated at it, who sits back from the table and looks askance as if unaware of its presence (Leblanc 1992: 68). He does not look at the camera, and it is impossible to say what the object of his

---

27 'If the Hôtel des Invalides hadn't been situated in Paris, if the Seine didn't run alongside, I'd never have shot *Hôtel des Invalides*. If the Lorraine steel works weren't surrounded by wheat fields, I'd never have shot *En passant par la Lorraine*' (Franju, quoted in Durgnat 1967: 19)

gaze is, if he is not just dreaming. The man of the second shot is dark and dressed in black, the woman blonde and wearing light-coloured clothes: his face is hidden from the camera, and as she kisses him hers is too. The shot is reminiscent of many a surrealist photograph of lovers, perhaps particularly in its association of erotic desire with blindness. Most important is that the couple have almost no connection to the rest of the film: in a section of a documentary conventionally devoted to establishing shots, this unconnected element is an emotional counterpoint to the subject of Franju's film, with the discontinuity provided by eroticism in contrast to the one represented by the brutality of the abattoir. Both these shots are firmly located geographically in the area that is Franju's 'subject', but through the technique of juxtaposition and disjuncture provide anything but a realistic presentation of it.

According to Leblanc, the technique Franju uses on the objects of his *courts métrages* can be broken down into three stages (Leblanc 1992: 17). First, the object is associated with the other images ('représentations audiovisuelles') that construct its interpretation: it is contextualised in a readily recognisable way. Second, in order to shift the standard interpretation viewers will be making of it, the object is detached from its usual context, enters an indeterminate space, and acquires an undecidable status. The viewer is temporarily at a loss as to how to look at and interpret the object being shown to him, but this changes again in the third stage, when the object is put into a new, less familiar context. It is now recontextualised, but still partly indeterminate: the signifying process set in train by its 'liberation' from a straightforward context continues to operate, as its context and discourses of interpretation are not sealed. This is the procedure of the 'insolite'.

Some extraordinary examples of this procedure are also to be found in the central section of *En passant par la Lorraine*, where Franju literally films the 'white heat of technology' in the Lorraine steel factories, and uses the industrial process as a kind of illustration of and metaphor for the decontextualisation and recontextualisation of the material object. Crumbling white-hot coal is seen passing along conveyor belts, and flows of molten metal pour forth from the immense pear-shaped concrete containers in which it has been smelted, and which breathe fire and flame as they tip to release their contents. Men use rakes, ladles and spades to clear the ground around the large-scale transfer of substances going on in these halls and chambers of smoke and fire. Franju's camera follows a block of hot, malleable metal right through the process of becoming an object: a huge, vertical, coffin-shaped ingot is lowered into a frame, wheeled away on rollers, then shaped to become a kind of long, slender girder. To the accompaniment of Maurice Jarre's eerie electronic music, the white-hot girder or cable is then threaded through a series of machines that repeatedly cast it forth and pull it in like a giant lasso. The outcome of this highly dangerous process (a skull-and-crossbones sign is visible in this zone of the factory) is a huge white plate of sheet-iron, but the molten metal is filmed mainly in its becoming: Franju's interest is unmistakably mainly in the ever-changing morphology of the object, which presents surreal and poetic images to the documentary viewer and resists all attempts to identify it as something known, defined and familiar.[28]

The work of a museum curator consists of recontextualising objects extracted from their natural context into a necessarily non-natural display. Leblanc's detailed commentary of *Hôtel des Invalides* reveals the similarity of Franju's film technique to curatorial work (which may explain the particular power of the documentary), and pays close attention to Franju's method of framing. According to Leblanc, Franju's frames in *Hôtel des Invalides* sometimes cut across the discourse of knowledge produced by the institution in order to appeal to the tourist – knowledge that ennobles and glorifies war. The wheelchair of a war veteran with a badly disfigured face is wheeled past a cannon so that it appears to be pointing at him – a framing of a person with an object that gives literal expression to the metaphor 'cannon fodder' (Leblanc 1992: 88). At another moment, the museum guide invites his visitors (and the documentary spectator) to look out through a window at the 'cour de la Victoire', and Franju utilises the frame made available by the action for his own purposes, showing not the disused war machinery the visitors are supposed to admire, but a winter scene of death and desolation that resembles an empty battlefield more than a museum. Franju's framing and camera angles create a look for the spectator that diverges from the look constructed by the guide, the official institutional view.

28 Franju commented later that it was obvious that the scenes of 'fonderie' (smelting) and 'laminage' (lamination) interested him the most in *En passant* (Brumagne 1977: 24–5).

The cinematic movement whose characteristic style relies most heavily on framing and staging is without doubt 1930s poetic realism, associated above all with the films of Marcel Carné. Durgnat pinpoints how Franju is able 'to "transform" locations, to endow them with the expressionistic intensity usually restricted to the big studio-set (the *locus classicus* being Carné's insistence on building an entire Métro station for *Les Portes de la Nuit* ...)' (Durgnat 1967: 9). A link is established here between expressionism and poetic realism that is not immediately obvious, since 'expressionism is traditionally considered as the negation of realism' (24). Franju's social interests and location filming might seem quite foreign to the staginess and constructed décors of German expressionism, but Murnau in fact

> anticipated Franju's gift for transforming locations: much of *Nosferatu* was filmed in the streets of Hamburg, and *Tabu* consists largely of location material. In France, the expressionistic urge was closely interwoven with realism: Jean Epstein turned from expressionism to documentaries in the 'twenties, and his *La Chute de la Maison Usher* intercuts expressionistic sets and location material to interesting effect. (25)

While one can see a figure such as Artaud as an expressionist very much in the German mould, 'French expressionism is lightened, or diluted, by impressionist interests and a more realistic strain (from French rationalism as against German romanticism)' (25). This explanation of Durgnat's offers a convincing explanation of Franju's heritage, even if it does not pursue the question of his perturbation of realism(s).

The opening section of *Le Sang des bêtes* provides some good examples of Franju's ability to 'artificialise' the real by framing and staging it, since his shots of the Ourcq canal and the gloomy buildings rising to either side of it are so photographic and precisely framed as to resemble stage sets, with which they also share a 'proscenium' iconography. Much later in the film a shot of a barge moving along the canal is framed so as to render the water invisible – the barge appears to be moving along the ground (stage) at the horizon, a shot Franju recomposes in *Les Poussières* by filming a barge gliding along a raised canal whose water is concealed behind an embankment. These effects might be termed 'surrealist', although the procedure behind them is probably nearer to the staginess and 'layering' of reality entailed by the complex studio designs of poetic realism. At this point any parallel between Franju and poetic realism runs out, however, since Franju nursed and often voiced a lifelong dislike of studios, to which he consistently preferred natural and location shooting (Borde 1961: 9; Bureau 1962: 6). Some scenes in his features were shot in the studio, of course, and most of *Nuits rouges* had to be for financial reasons, but as the *long métrage* décors I described and reviewed at the start of this chapter quickly reveal, location settings in villas, castles, ruins, and bourgeois and rural dwellings predominate. Franju was a great admirer of the poetic realist movement, and on occasion enthused about studio cinema, but what excited him about the latter was a constructedness or 'artificialism' he did not need to have built (at great expense), because he already saw it in the natural reality that surrounded him, exterior and interior. The technique at work in *Le Sang des bêtes* I described on page 122 relates specifically to the difference between 'outside' and 'inside' realities, and consists of representing 'natural' reality as a construct, of making exterior shots appear to be interior ones. This was a constructedness at which Franju was deliberately aiming, since he said of his first documentary 'nous avons cherché dans notre film à restituer au réel documentaire son apparence d'artifice et au décor naturel son propre aspect de décor planté' (Franju typescript, published in Maison de la Villette 1992: 13–15).[29] It was entirely consistent with his dislike of studios. In the end, then, Franju's perturbation of realistic presentation is something quite distinct from poetic realist 'artificialism', whose grand designs it never attempts to imitate; his technique of *re*composing the real through framing, photography and the position of the camera simply shows that it is always already composed, and reconstructable in a myriad of visually impressive ways.

29 'in our film we sought to return its appearance of artifice to the documentary real, and to give back to a natural location its proper look of a constructed set'.

References

Armes, Roy (1985), *French Cinema*, Oxford, Oxford University Press.

Aumont, Jacques (1992), *Du visage au cinéma*, Paris, Editions de l'Etoile.

Aumont, Jacques (sous la direction de) (1995), *L'Invention de la figure humaine: le cinéma: l'humain et l'inhumain*, Paris, Cinémathèque française.

Bazin, André (1983), 'Le Film scientifique: beauté du hasard', in *Le Cinéma français de la Libération à la Nouvelle Vague (1945–58)*, textes réunis et préfacés par Jean Narboni, Paris, Cahiers du cinéma and Editions de l'Etoile, pp. 220–2.

Borde, Raymond (1961), 'Georges Franju et le réalisme poétique' (interview), *Image et Son* 146 (December), 8–10.

Brumagne, Marie-Madeleine (1977), *Georges Franju. Impressions et aveux*, Lausanne, l'Age d'Homme.

Buache, Freddy (1955), 'Les premiers films de Georges Franju', *Positif* 13 (March–April), 33–5.

Buache, Freddy (1996), *Georges Franju: poésie et vérité*, Paris, Cinémathèque française.

Bureau, Patrick (1962), 'Entretien avec Georges Franju', *Contre-champ* 4 (October), 5–8.

Chevrie, Marc (1986), 'Les figures de la peur' (interview), *Cahiers du cinéma* 389 (November), 45–7.

Durgnat, Raymond (1967), *Franju*, London, Studio Vista.

Ezra, Elizabeth (2000), *Georges Méliès*, Manchester, Manchester University Press,

Frayling, Christopher (2000), 'They're bad, mad and dangerous to know', *The Times Higher Education Supplement*, 8 September, 18–19.

Freeland, Cynthia A. (1998), 'Realist horror', in Carolyn Korsmeyer (ed.), *Aesthetics: The Big Questions*, Malden MA and Oxford, Blackwell, pp. 283–94.

Gauthier, Guy (1995), *Le Documentaire, un autre cinéma*, Paris, Editions Nathan.

Gibbs, John (2002), *Mise en scène. Film Style and Interpretation*, London, Wallflower Press.

Leblanc, Gérard (1992), *Une esthétique de la déstabilisation*, Paris, Maison de la Villette.

Lebovits, Jean-Marc and Tranchant, François (1959), 'Entretien avec Georges Franju cinéaste et poète du merveilleux quotidien', *Cinéma* 34 (March), 16–25.

Porcile, François (1965), *Défense du court métrage français*, Paris, Les Editions du Cerf.

Siclier, Jacques (1987), 'Le fantastique social', *Le Monde* 15 April.

Vialle, Gabriel (1968), *Georges Franju*, Paris, Seghers.

4

Surviving the reign of the father: gender, the family and eroticism

In this final chapter I shall examine the female characters in Franju's cinema, their relationships with male characters, and the structure of the family in his films. Also incorporated in these discussions will be the relationships of which the family is forged, and the eroticism to be found in Franju's film narratives and in his aesthetic syntax. To date there has been no sustained attempt by either francophone or anglophone film critics to address these areas, which, although predictable when viewed as part of the critical neglect that has dogged Franju's work since 1970, is surprising from the standpoint of the wealth of writing in gender studies that has grown up over the same period. Franju's films are in fact populated with interesting female characters, marked by complex family dynamics, and contain some suggestively (though rarely explicitly) erotic moments. These traits occur particularly in his feature films, but what I shall argue to be the prevalent tendency in his representation of gender and male–female relationships is established early, in two of his *courts métrages*. I shall start, therefore, by returning to *Monsieur et Madame Curie* and *La Première Nuit*.

Gender, society and politics

As noted in Chapter 1 and remarked upon by most of the film's critics from the 1950s on, Franju's biographical sketch of Marie and Pierre Curie is as much a love story as an account of the discovery of radioactivity by two of the twentieth century's most important scientists. Equally striking in the film, however, is the image it creates of a serene and highly productive professional partnership. This is evoked by all the laboratory sequences that make up the greater part of the fourteen-minute short, in which Marie and Pierre move silently around their lab with seemingly infinite patience and grace. The absence of live dialogue in the film creates the impression that they have no need of verbal communication, so good is their understanding of each other's actions and expressions. This mutuality and reciprocal harmony in a male–female relationship clearly does not imply equal professional recognition (we are told that it is Pierre who is rewarded by being appointed as Professor of Physics at the Institut de France) or complete equality of gender roles, since when the Curies' children appear with them in the short final pastoral scene, the children are closer to Marie than Pierre, suggesting she is more involved in caring for them than her husband. But the images Franju constructs are of equality-in-difference, in which men and women are psychologically equal beings, and women are most definitely 'subjects' in their own right. Franju once commented on female subjectivity in the context of an exchange about the rise of female stars in 1950s French and Hollywood cinema, suggesting that the 'femme-spectacle' (Brigitte Bardot, Marilyn Monroe) might be called the 'femme-objet', against which the 'femme-sujet' should be defined as the 'femme psychologique' (Brumagne 1977: 55). The 'psychological', meditative woman really belonged to literature and, although out of vogue from the 1950s on, would in Franju's view return to cinema when it was once again able to 'hear her language' (55). Thérèse Desqueyroux was an example of this type of woman, and Franju was attracted to her character because she combined a meditative nature with worldly agency (Borde 1962: 62).

This psychological and human equality of women to men is illustrated especially well in the sequence of *Monsieur et Madame Curie* where the Curies have ordered tonnes of pitchblende, the principal source of uranium and radium, to be dissolved in boiling liquid as part of their experiments. Work takes place in the courtyard of the Ecole de Physique because harmful gases are not allowed in their laboratory, and up to twenty kilograms of solids are boiled up at a time, 'un travail exténuant'.[1] Marie, the woman and member of the physically 'weaker' sex, is shown doing the lion's share of the heavy work of stirring the steaming cauldron. The reason for this is not

1 'exhausting work'.

explained, but the camera lingers on her accomplished labour with an unmistakable pathos that goes some way towards righting the disequilibrium between men's and women's work shown in the scene. Although injustice exists in the roles men and women are expected to fulfil, representation contributes to correcting this imbalance: Marie Curie is in the frame far more than Pierre, and it is her words (the scientist turned writer) that, read by Nicole Stéphane, contribute the film's commentary. The inequality between the sexes is recorded in Franju's film, and in a way that endorses a metaphysical binary opposition between femaleness and materiality, but Franju does this with almost complete neutrality, and with a choice of scenes and composition that privileges femininity-in-representation. Furthermore, the humanism of his camerawork leans towards the woman in his story. Male and female roles are differentiated according to gender, but are seen to be of complementary and equal (although different) value.

The second of Franju's *courts métrages* to observe this type of complementarity and equality between the sexes is his last, *La Première Nuit*. A story of first love and separation, its urban, underground setting and Eugen Shuftan's eerie photography give it a poetic atmosphere reinforced by the dramatisation of the protagonist's dream that occupies its central section. At the start of the film, the boy has arrived in a chauffeured car at his school just as a blonde girl of about his age emerges from the Métro into which he is to descend. She turns towards him, and he smiles at her from the car; she then smiles back as she passes. Once the boy is in the Métro, the start of his dream is signalled by his walking down the rising escalator on which he has in fact just fallen asleep. An apparently empty train moves through the station he finds himself in, but the girl then appears in one carriage of the train, although she does not see or look at him. The train passes a second time, upon which she smiles and looks fondly at him, and he starts to run along the platform with the passing train. With his head in his hands and tears running down his cheeks, he looks up to her as her train moves away, bowing his head again as the ghost-like vision of her disappears. An empty train then stops at the station, and a set of doors opens for him to get in. The doors into the adjoining carriage close as if shutting him out (enclosing him within the one carriage), and another train containing the girl passes his. After a short moment in which the children are face to face, but with their eyes scarcely meeting, the tracks on which the two trains are travelling bifurcate, the girl's disappearing into a tunnel at a higher level. Tears are again visible on the boy's face at this point; this is a sorrowful parting.

La Première Nuit is dedicated 'à ceux qui n'ont pas renié leur enfance':[2] adults who retain the capacity to imagine (or dream) with the same vigour as children do – such as the boy in Franju's film. Given its themes of attraction and separation, and the overdetermin-able symbolism of moving trains that suggest sexual drives or desire, *La Première Nuit* seems to invite a psychoanalytic reading. However, if one attempts to locate Freudian Oedipality in the film, or any of the Imaginary or Symbolic structures proposed by Lacanian psycho-analysis, one does not get very far. No fusional desiring relationship is present to be broken up, as in Freud's accounts of the transition from the Oedipus to the castration complexes (or vice versa for the little girl); there is no play between duality and the triangulation of Lacan's Symbolic order. The boy reawakens as the escalator he has slept on starts up again early in the morning, rubs his eyes and goes out into the daylight, wending his way along a river or canal through a misty park, presumably towards home. Despite the power of his dream and the sorrow he is shown feeling in it, there is no sense of trauma, and nothing in the 'Métro' narrative links up to his family relationships or events in his life, beyond the real existence of his blonde classmate. If any psychoanalytic theory can meaningfully be mapped onto *La Première Nuit*, it is probably the kind of object relations theory that proposes a subjectivity for the infant from its earliest days. Although clearly not independent in terms of care and socialisation, the child in this type of psychology is from the start a 'subject' capable of forming relations with 'objects' (other people). In Franju's film, it is surely telling that during the wordless encounter between the boy and his remote, cool, blonde schoolmate, their trains travel on separate, parallel tracks. Since both boy and girl are on the verge of adolescence, *La Première Nuit* does not offer any commentary on the roles of men and women in society, or the equality or inequality between them. But, like *Monsieur et Madame Curie*, it contributes to a vision of gender relations in which both men and women are fully fledged, separate subjects and psychological beings.

Franju's vision of women's place in society and his tendency to focus on women as the objects and subjects of representation can be

2 'those who have not renounced their childhood'.

directly related to the political inclinations that mark many of his films. As Leblanc emphasises when writing about *Hôtel des Invalides* and *Les Poussières*, Franju's depiction of the disfiguring effects of war and the uncalculated harm inflicted by industrial work always remains at the level of diagnosis, and never enters into explicit politico-historical criticism or the proposing of solutions. In narrative terms, this means that Franju stops short of displaying the suffering of the victim, where 'victims' can be defined (as François Chevassu does), as 'those who do not have the right to be freely themselves':

> Ces victimes jalonnent tous ses films: Heurtevent et François (*La Tête contre les murs*), Anne et Thérèse (*Thérèse Desqueyroux*), Christiane (*Les Yeux sans visage*), Jacqueline (*Judex*), Roy, Thomas et Pajot (*Thomas l'imposteur*), etc., mais aussi, plus anonymes mais non moins présents, les victimes de la guerre d'*Hôtel des Invalides*, les ouvriers d'*En passant par la Lorraine*, les pollués de *Poussières*, les aliénés de *La Tête contre les murs*, les soldats de *Thomas l'imposteur*, etc.: jusqu'aux animaux: ceux, torturés, du *Sang des bêtes*, celui, abandonné et gazé, de *Mon chien*, les palombes piégées de *Thérèse Desqueyroux*, les saumons d'*A propos d'une rivière* et, les symbolisant tous, peut-être, le cheval enflammé de *Thomas l'imposteur*, victime parmi les victimes.[3] (Chevassu 1988: 71)

In Franju's cinema, 'victims' appear in human and animal collectivities and as the main protagonists of his narratives. Franju's political leanings are humanist ones: they do not embrace any particular ideology and are not translatable into the party-political system of any country. He is always and only concerned to point out inequality and suffering, and to suggest that these derive from the lack of liberty of the individual(s) concerned.

Although passionate about injustice and the inequities produced by social institutions and power relations at work within them, then, Franju does not explicitly politicise his film narratives. His lack of

3 'These victims serve as markers in all his films: Heurtevent and François (*La Tête contre les murs*), Anne and Thérèse (*Thérèse Desqueyroux*), Christiane (*Les Yeux sans visage*), Jacqueline (*Judex*), Roy, Thomas and Pajot (*Thomas l'imposteur*), etc., but also, anonymous but no less present, the war victims of *Hôtel des Invalides*, the workers of *En passant par la Lorraine* and *Les Poussières*, the mental patients of *La Tête contre les murs*, the soldiers of *Thomas l'imposteur*, etc.: right down to the animals: those tortured in *Le Sang des bêtes*, the dog abandoned and gassed in *Mon chien*, the trapped doves in *Thérèse Desqueyroux*, the salmon of *A propos d'une rivière* and, symbolising them all, perhaps, the horse with its mane on fire in *Thomas l'imposteur*, victim among victims.'

interest in so doing is entirely in harmony with the views he occa-
sionally expressed about the relationship – or non-relationship – of art
to politics, since when asked in the wake of the 1968 *événements* about
cinema's links with revolution, he replied with characteristic blunt-
ness 'C'est très con! Il n'a jamais rien fait, le cinéma. Il a toujours suivi
la révolution. Toujours. Même chez Eisenstein. Pouvez-vous me citer
un film, un seul, qui ait fait la révolution quelque part?' (Gauteur
1970: 77).[4] In France, 1968 could not be considered as any kind of
political revolution, because in his view revolutions always come
about 'pour des raison *vitales*',[5] and many of the students initiating the
1968 events were from bourgeois backgrounds and would in due
course go on to be lawyers, doctors and 'PDGs' (managing directors).
In Franju's view cinema could only record and follow political change,
not instigate it, and he clearly had little sympathy with the concept of
'engagement' or the attaching of any political programme to the
activity of film-making. (The one instance in which he may have
departed from this belief is his adaptation of Zola's *La Faute de l'Abbé
Mouret*, to which I shall return at the end of this chapter.) Art (cinema)
could certainly have humanist political content and point out suffering and injustice, but it should not be harnessed to political ends.

Franju's humanist tendency always to sympathise with the victim
is closely linked to his dislike of and discomfort with certain important social institutions, principally the Church and the army. His
passionate disapproval of war is evident throughout *Hôtel des Invalides*,
and the senselessness and arbitrariness of military combat already
focused on by Cocteau in *Thomas l'Imposteur* is enhanced by cinematography and the inventive uses to which he puts light and fire in his
adaptation. Franju's anti-clericalism became well known – indeed,
took on quasi-mythic proportions – after his inclusion in *Le Sang des
bêtes* of a few shots of two nuns visiting the abattoirs to scavenge for
spare animal parts not even yet transformed into cuts of meat,
although it had to wait until his 1970 adaptation of *La Faute de l'Abbé
Mouret* to find its fullest expression. Critics have repeatedly emphasised Franju's non-conformist and critical attitude to the Church and
the army, but one institution to which they have never devoted any

4 'That's rubbish! Cinema has never done anything, it's always followed revolution, always. Even with Eisenstein. Can you name me one single film that has
   brought about revolution, anywhere?'
5 'for *vital* reasons'.

analysis is the family – which in Franju's feature films means the patriarchal family. Although they are also victims in other ways, the protagonists of *La Tête contre les murs*, *Les Yeux sans visage*, *Thérèse Desqueyroux* and *Judex* are principally, strikingly, victims of the patriarchal family – of the inflexibility, corruption, cruelty or limitations of a father or husband figure. Is the patriarchal family an institution comparable to other institutions, a social formation like the Church and the army, which have themselves been differently modified by the evolving gender roles and sexualities of the second half of the twentieth century? This is a huge sociological question, and its scope considerably exceeds Franju's cinema. What I shall concentrate on in the next section, though, is the persistence of the patriarchal family's structure in Franju's narratives, and the suggestion his plot-writing repeatedly seems to make that any family governed by an immutable paternal law is an uncaring and corrupt one.

The family and the law

The four of Franju's films that dramatise particularly meaningfully the limitations and violences enacted by a patriarchal family structure are, as I noted above, *La Tête contre les murs*, *Les Yeux sans visage*, *Thérèse Desqueyroux* and *Judex*. All four of these films lend themselves to being read with the tools of a type of feminist approach dominant in women's and gender studies in the 1980s, a psychoanalytically oriented criticism that drew particularly on Freud's accounts of the construction of sexual difference and Lacan's concepts of the Imaginary and Symbolic orders. According to this type of approach, masculinity and femininity are constructed 'fictions' achieved at a price by the small boys and girls whose sexuality is exposed in the Oedipal structure of the patriarchal family: while the little boy moves from an Oedipal relationship with his mother to a 'crisis' of (threatened, fantasised) castration in a rivalrous relationship with his father, the little girl progresses from a castration complex implying actual castration (the lack of a penis) into an Oedipally triangular structure where she may (if she does not marry) remain locked in rivalry with her mother for her father's affections and desires. These clearly differentiated trajectories of masculinity and femininity are somewhat blurred by Lacan's concepts of the Imaginary and Symbolic orders, which apply to both male and female children, and describe a shift from a phase of dual, dyadic relationships (the Imaginary order corresponds roughly to Freud's 'pre-Oedipal' stage in so far as the child is locked in a relationship with its mother, although it perceives its own identity as a body, and its difference from the world around it) to triadic, triangulated ones. In Lacan's terminology, entry into the Symbolic order is effected by an encounter with the paternal law which, crucially for Lacanian theory, involves entry into language. Lacan's 'return' to Freud renewed and transformed Freudian narratives of the construction of sexual difference by combining his ideas with structural linguistics: in Lacanian theory, the phallus is a signifier, and another term for the paternal law is the 'Name of the Father' (the 'nom du père', where 'nom' is a homonym of 'non', no). To Freud's concepts of the Oedipus and castration complexes Lacan's structural orders (entry into the Symbolic is definitive except in cases of psychosis) add the status of a transcendental law that exceeds any single instantiation in which it is experienced by a human subject. Lacan's description of the apparatus that constructs human sexuality and identity may initially appear to offer more equality to little girls alongside little boys, since the Imaginary and Symbolic orders do not interact with children's unorganised sexuality in a way that differentiates the masculine and the feminine as clearly as Freud's accounts do, but the Lacanian Symbolic is quite clearly phallocentric, that is, biased towards the phallus and the masculine.

Before discussing those of Franju's feature films in which the patriarchal family – and seemingly, therefore, a phallocentric Symbolic order – is the central structure, I shall look briefly at *Thomas l'Imposteur*, which differs from this pattern. Cocteau's novel and Franju's film adaptation are in part a family drama, in which the family in question consists, at least to start with, just of a mother and her daughter, the Princesse de Bormes and Henriette. This is no father-dominated family, since the Princesse is an independent and eligible widow, but the plot of *Thomas* involves some very Oedipal dynamics. It is to the Princesse that Thomas first poses as the nephew of General de Fontenoy, and by so doing he becomes first part of her band of war 'helpers' – the ambulance convoy that travels into German-occupied territory – and quickly a kind of adoptive son, giving incestuous overtones to the relationship that slowly develops between Thomas and the frail and delicate Henriette (one which echoes the brother–

sister incest of Cocteau's poetic novel *Les Enfants terribles*, written not long after *Thomas l'Imposteur* in 1929 and famously adapted for the cinema by Jean-Pierre Melville in 1949). A triangulation is set up around the character of Thomas that is not at all traditionally Oedipal, since mother and daughter are competing for the affections of the son. They do not do this openly, but after Thomas' true identity is discovered and he is sent away to the Belgian front both appear to miss him equally, and accept with alacrity the opportunity to visit him created by the Princesse's chief admirer Pesquel-Duport. A second, much more traditional Oedipal triangulation is set up around the character of the Princesse, involving Thomas and Pesquel-Duport, who professes envy of her affection for the boy-soldier. Apparently quite content with her status as desirable widow, the Princesse is particularly firm with Pesquel-Duport, whom she puts down with the characteristically formal and negatively formulated (and intoned) sentence 'De tous mes admirateurs vous êtes celui qui me déplaît le moins'.[6] Despite the markedly Oedipal character of these relationship patterns, however, and the link made between Oedipality and narrative by both Freud and many psychoanalytic literary critics, feminist and non-feminist, the final outcome of *Thomas l'Imposteur* is not propelled by them. Thomas meets his death on his way to pick up a message that he never discovers is a love letter from Henriette, and she sickens and dies two months later in a sanatorium, from 'une maladie nerveuse qui n'était pas mortelle'[7] – explained by Cocteau to mean that she poisoned herself (one of the closing images of Franju's film is her empty invalid's bed). *Thomas l'Imposteur* is therefore left without its 'children', and with a couple of 'parent' figures who are not a true couple, a picture of non-fulfilment very typical of the negativity and indeterminate sexuality that figures in so many of Cocteau's images and narratives, across all the media for which he wrote.

So the family dynamics of *Thomas l'Imposteur* are, if not positive, much more open than those of *La Tête contre les murs*, *Les Yeux sans visage*, *Thérèse Desqueyroux* and *Judex*, an openness that can be put down to Franju's fidelity to the narrative of Cocteau's novel. Interestingly, with all the other four films I am discussing under the rubric of 'the family', Franju either altered the source story from which he was working, or (in the case of *Thérèse Desqueyroux*) took a different view

6 'Of all my admirers, you are the one I dislike the least'.
7 'a non-fatal nervous illness'.

of the fortunes of his female protagonist by refusing to endorse Mauriac's sequel to his novel. Since *La Tête contre les murs* and *Les Yeux sans visage* are only loosely based on the novels from which they were drawn, it is telling that the 'adaptation' (from a film rather than a book in this instance) Franju altered the most with respect to the family is the one in which the law is most clearly associated with a masculine protagonist, in the figure and name of 'Judex', the judge or 'law-giver'.

As I set out in Chapter 2, Franju's adaptation of Feuillade's serial entirely omits the history that gives Judex his motivation for seeking revenge on Favraux, responsible for Judex's father's suicide through having ruined him financially. Franju thus leaves out an entire Oedipally oriented history from his film in order to render it less 'plotty' and more visually poetic, and to give more mystery to Judex's character. In so doing he completely omits the world of masculine competition over business and success, considerably softening the vision of cut-throat male rivalry that dominates both Feuillade's *Judex* and his earlier *Fantômas*. (It is significant, however, that Favraux remains a killer of fathers, through his attempted murder of Kerjean, the old man who turns out to be the father of Diana Monti's lover–assistant Moralès.) In Franju's *Judex*, his chief character's main motivation for kidnapping Favraux is to rescue Jacqueline, and in view of this shift in characterisation (Judex becomes an ineffectual hero who eventually achieves his aim as much through accident as through design) and Franju's partial transfer of narrative agency to Diana Monti, it is fair to say that he 'feminises' Feuillade's narrative to a considerable degree. The other way in which *Judex* attenuates and problematises masculinity is not of Franju's making, since it is a narrative element also found in Feuillade; this is the division of Judex's character into the dark, handsome, dashing figure he cuts *as* Judex and his second identity as the grey-haired, doddering old butler Vallières. Franju's comments on Judex's behaviour that I quoted in Chapter 2 – that his techniques are fully as 'sadistic' as Favraux's – show that Franju was aware of the moral ambiguity of the law that Judex represents. But this ambiguity extends not only to oppositions between youth versus age and 'spectacle' (Judex's magic tricks) versus secrecy (Vallières' identity is only revealed late in the film), but to the very figure of the law itself, which is rendered unstable by being divided in two. It is difficult to state with conviction that the law figured by the character(s) of Judex is a paternal law of the kind that structures Lacan's Symbolic order, since neither Judex nor Vallières is actually a father. The coincidence of the identity of law-giver with Judex's name certainly supports the notion of a linguistically oriented masculinity, and both Feuillade's and Franju's films associate masculinity firmly with the law. But although both films end happily, this is because of a fortunate narrative outcome for the female protagonist Jacqueline and for the Judex–Jacqueline couple, not because of any modification to the uncertain identity of Judex. In Franju's as in Feuillade's *Judex*, the figure of the law is divided and unstable and the fortunes of the family uncertain, and there is little in either film to suggest the inevitable prevalence of a fixed, immutable or transcendent Law of the Father.

The same cannot be said of the family and institutional dynamics that structure the narrative of Franju's first feature *La Tête contre les murs*, which I read in Chapter 2 as a bleak and unrelieved *film noir*. François Gérane suffers his fate of internment in a psychiatric asylum at the hands of no less than three institutions – the family, the law of the land, and the institution of medicine – and the powers that these three structures wield over his life overlap in several ways. So it is because of petty crime committed against his father – the theft of some money and the burning of some official papers M. Gérane should not have brought home – that François is interned in the first place, according to a law that allows this to be done on the authority of a family doctor, a law of which François is unaware. M. Gérane requests that this be done based on knowledge gained in his career as a senior lawyer, and he does so in front of François, who rashly seems to consider that his father would not use the law against his own son, because it would damage his reputation. François' relationship with his father is thus an entirely negative one, and as he commits his crime he is already an outlaw in his family, having gained access to his father's turreted mansion by jumping over its wall and finding an unlocked door that does not require the key he presumably does not have.

François' residence in a rural asylum of 'aliénés' away from Paris brings him into contact with two further figures of male authority, the doctors Varmont (Pierre Brasseur) and Emery (Paul Meurisse), psychiatrists who espouse entirely contrasting views of how to treat the mentally ill. (Little actual treatment of patients apart from the dispensing of sedating injections is seen in *La Tête contre les murs*, but in some group scenes of the inmates' behaviour and in the debate about psychiatric methods staged by the differences between Varmont and Emery, the film does have, as I commented earlier, a strongly topical – for 1958 – and documentary component.) Although not a cruel man, Varmont holds the view that the first duty of psychiatry is not to help or cure the patient, but to protect the public, which makes him a staunch upholder of permanent internment, even in cases of such minor 'delinquency' as François'. During his initial assessment of François, he shines a light in his eyes, questions him roughly and aggressively, and listens to only a few words of response before declaring him 'unstable', and suffering from 'troubles de comport-ment et de caractère'.[8] A little later, he sums up François' problems as '[un] bel exemple de haine contre le père',[9] as if this were in itself a pathology. Emery, by contrast, is reputed for taking an interest in his patients' personalities, and believes the vast majority of France's 120,000 mental patients could be cured, given the right treatment. His methods involve encouraging them to take up creative activities (he proudly demonstrates indications of recovery in the symbols of life they have modelled in clay) and the proscription of punishment of any kind, such as is inflicted on François when he attempts escape for the second time (he is shot in the leg). In a head-to-head discussion between Varmont and Emery that takes place just after this, Emery asks to be allowed to take François on as a patient, but is refused by a Varmont displaying unmistakable signs of paternal possessiveness. When he repeats to Emery his belief that patients such as François must be locked away in order to protect society, Emery responds 'La police est là pour ça':[10] Varmont uses his power to intern François as if he were a police officer and a judge as well as a doctor.

Most chillingly, however, Varmont is a substitute authoritarian father for François, a role made clear in a scene where he slowly injects him with a barbiturate to put him to sleep, questioning him in the meantime about his relationship with his parents, and using an extremely condescending 'we' mode of address to refer to actions only his patient has carried out. The music that accompanies this scene (like the rest of the music for *La Tête contre les murs*, composed by Maurice Jarre) is a simple nursery-style piano melody that otherwise only plays as François breaks into his father's house. It clearly

8 'behavioural and character difficulties'.
9 'a fine example of hatred of the father'.
10 'That's what the police are for'.

identifies Varmont's ministerings to François as those of a father lulling his son to sleep – but in a most sinister manner. And the story it accompanies is even more sinister, since from François' account of his mother's death, which occurred when he was eight, it appears that his father might have murdered her. As François tells it, his father informed some acquaintances that his mother drowned in a pond in the grounds of their property, but told others (including his son, who was looking out through a window at the time) that she had committed suicide. François recounts that his mother used to scream when his father touched her and cry when he talked to her, behaviour that sounds like that of a woman who has suffered violence. And although François saw his father lead his mother back towards the pond where she met her death, his father claimed later that she had been alone. This suspicious if inconclusive narrative is investigated a little further in questions Varmont puts to M. Gérane on the one occasion he visits his son in the asylum, but the doctor is quickly reassured by Gérane's corroboration of his wife's suicide by drowning, and by learning that the matter was not considered questionable enough to merit a legal inquiry. Varmont declares himself happy that Gérane suffered no more than slander, and the exchange leaves an impression of a mutually reinforcing and self-satisfied world of male professionals concerned only to protect its own interests.

Metaphorically speaking, then, *La Tête contre les murs* features three fathers, two of whom are 'bad' and one who is good (or better), but powerless to help François: in the psychiatric system in which Varmont and Emery work, neither of them can choose their patients. (Despite his sympathy and liberal views, Emery also fails to help François' friend Heurtevent, who commits suicide after their failed escape attempt and repeated refused requests to be taken on as Emery's patient.) The world of Franju's film is a bleakly masculinist one, in which the law and society itself, through its institutional representatives, will not tolerate any derogation from its severely imposed rules. This equation of society with the law is made explicit by M. Gérane when he visits François in the asylum, and says that society is a game whose rules must be observed. François admits that he has never had much interest in so doing, to which his father replies that he would try the patience of a saint. But whatever François' misdemeanours, his punishment is out of proportion, since the odds have been stacked against him from the start. M. Gérane is a severe and ungenerous parent, and also seemingly an outright misogynist, who accuses his late wife of violence, cruelty and bad faith, and objects even to François' girlfriend Stéphanie visiting him. Apart from Stéphanie, whose implication in François' fate is minimal, there are no female characters in *La Tête contre les murs* against whom his misogyny can be measured, but it lingers as a malevolent force in the film, reinforcing its *film noir* characteristics. More importantly for the film's protagonist, paternity and the family are associated with a restrictive and unloving law that expects more from its children than it ever gives, and punishes them for failing to comply.

The narrative of *La Tête contre les murs* might well be described as illustrating a phallocentric Symbolic order, then, and offers much to an analysis of masculinities. However, the most important challenges to phallogocentrism are usually posed by female narrative agents, and this is as true of Franju's cinema as it is generally. I shall therefore devote the rest of this section to readings of the two of his films that feature independent and rebellious female characters: *Thérèse Desqueyroux* and *Les Yeux sans visage*. What part do the patriarchal family and the paternal law play in these two films?

Thérèse Desqueyroux is not an unambiguously feminist heroine, since as Thérèse tries for a final time to explain to her husband Bernard as she bids him farewell at a Paris café in Franju's film, 'il y a deux Thérèses'.[11] The first is the bourgeois property-owning Thérèse who marries into the Desqueyroux family to assure the union of two pine forests, and genuinely belongs to her class and region of upbringing; the second is the independent, intellectual Thérèse who is stifled by life in the Landes region and marriage, and not suited to motherhood. At the end of both novel and film the second Thérèse gets her chance to live an independent life in Paris in the apartment Bernard pays for in order to maintain her health and hush up the scandal of her attempt to poison him, but her freedom is only acquired after a close encounter with the law, during the trial she undergoes for her crime. Her closest contact with the law as institution is in fact in the person of Bernard, a qualified lawyer, but this aspect of his identity hardly figures in Franju's film, where it takes a definite second place to his obsession with property and propriety. The association of the law with masculinity in *Thérèse Desqueyroux*, and

11 'there are two Thérèses'.

the encounter with it by a woman aspiring to freedom, is once again suggestive in relation to Lacan's phallocentric Symbolic order, but as in *Judex*, the law proves to have no real power or authority. The verdict at Thérèse's trial is a 'non-lieu', a non-verdict that comes about because Bernard, fearful of the damaging effect gossip about Thérèse's crime would have on his family and his reputation, declines to testify against her. Both the institution of the law itself and Bernard as its symbolic and actual representative (a lawyer and her husband) prove to be completely ineffectual: the 'non-lieu' that ends Thérèse's trial figures an aporia of the law, a suspension of judgment that leaves Thérèse's guilt and responsibility for her actions uncertain. And if Mauriac revealed his discomfort with this ending by returning to the character of Thérèse in his later novel *La Fin de la nuit*, Franju declined so to do, and stated publicly his preference for the spirited, independent Thérèse granted her freedom at the end of *Thérèse Desqueyroux*.

The feminist reading offered by the narrative of *Les Yeux sans visage* is a more complex one, and only one of multiple interpretations the film offers, many of which are intertextually linked to other stories and films. A recent approach (Hawkins 2000: 65–85) sees it as an allegory of events in European history, either of Nazi imperialism (Dr Genessier's blockhouse-surgery as concentration-camp 'sanitorium') or of France's Algerian war, underway at the time the film was made (here, Dr Genessier's torturer–victim relationship with his daughter Christiane becomes an analogue of the relationship of colonial to colonised power, including the actual torture of Algerian freedom fighters by the French military). The way to these approaches may have been opened by reviews such as Bruno Gay-Lussac's in *L'Express* of 10 March 1960, in which he suggested that *Les Yeux sans visage* was not a horror film but 'une histoire fabuleuse de la mythologie moderne'.[12] Such readings are not mutually exclusive and can all claim their share of validity; however, in view of the centrality of the character of Christiane Genessier to the film's narrative, and her audacious act of revolt with which it closes, it is astonishing that no feminist reading focused on her entrapment and subsequent freedom has ever been attempted.[13]

12 'a fabulous story of modern mythology'.
13 It is also interesting that a recent article (Bowman 2002) on the film claiming that it is 'without politics' declares that viewers 'should hesitate ... to consider [Christiane] a reliable source of information about her father', while maintaining

At the end of *Les Yeux sans visage*, Christiane cuts free Paulette Mérodon (the police's 'plant' in their investigation of Genessier) from the operating table, then with the same scalpel, the instrument of her father's regime, stabs Louisa (Alida Valli), her father's assistant and perhaps his lover, in the neck. Apparently uncomprehending and offended, Louisa croaks 'Pourquoi ça?'[14] as her eyes fill with tears and she slides to the floor. Christiane then moves into the tunnel-shaped extension to her father's secret operating theatre housing the dogs on which he practises his surgical experiments, and releases them from their cages one by one. As they bound outside to freedom, Genessier approaches from the villa's grounds, and the dogs go for him, pulling at his arms, mauling him, and finally leaving him motionless on the ground with a bloody, ruined face. It is important that although Christiane brings about and may be said to be responsible for her father's death, she is not the agent of his destruction or of the termination of his unethical surgical procedures: this is effected by his animal 'slaves' in their revolution against Genessier's tyranny. Christiane's act can be read in similarly political terms: it is too late for humanity to be restored to her in the shape of a viewable face (Genessier's transplant surgery has failed), but not too late to arrest the repeated violence being done to other young women abducted to her father's villa, in the appalling traffic in human faces set up by his illicit operations. Christiane acts for other women, not just for herself.[15] She also

---

that Louisa's word 'is at least as good as Christiane's'. According to Bowman, the only reliable testimony about Genessier's character we have is that he loves his daughter. I would disagree categorically with this: we know a great deal about Christiane's relationship with her father, and nothing prevents us making a feminist reading that identifies with her point of view.

14 'Why do that?'

15 As Elizabeth Cowie (2002) notes in her ethical reading of the film, Christiane's action in choosing to free Paulette and other, future victims 'is figured by Franju's closing images as also her freedom for herself'. In Cowie's reading, Christiane's ethical choice is 'not only – and perhaps not even primarily – her action to prevent another girl's defacement', because it is also a choice to accept her self as mutilated, 'to turn away from the fascination with the beautiful constituted for her by her father's desire'. My reading differs from Cowie's Lacanian one in the greater emphasis I am placing on otherness (selflessness) in feminine desire: I agree that Christiane acts in part for herself, but consider her act to be ethically femin*ist* (rather than just femin*ine*) because its primary aim is to prevent the defacement of other (future) women.

acts against the results of her father's will to power (her disfigurement is the result of a road accident caused by her father's 'besoin de dominer'[16]), and it is clear from the way Franju choreographs and films the dogs' revenge on Genessier – the first dog to attack him paws repeatedly at his crotch – that his inhumanity is 'phallocentric'.

In my view, the resonance and significance of Christiane's revolt is best understood in relation to the Frankenstein myth it resembles (many commentators have noted this), and can only fully be appreciated when gender (which plays a significant part in the Frankenstein story) is taken into account. The links of *Les Yeux sans visage* to Mary Shelley's *Frankenstein* and its many cinematic transformations lie not in Genessier's status as the stereotypical 'mad scientist' of horror film, an identity assumed even by critics as subtle and wide-ranging as Durgnat (as I argued in Chapter 3, Genessier is a guilty and desperate criminal, but also quite sane and genuinely concerned for his daughter); they should be located, rather, in Christiane's status as monster or Genessier's 'creature', and in the iconography of the figure of Louisa. Louisa too has suffered disfigurement of some kind, and been 'repaired' by Genessier. She is loyal to him because he has saved her 'face', and kind to Christiane as a fellow-victim of injury to appearance; it is because she understands only loyalty and not its wider implications that she cannot comprehend Christiane's revolt. To disguise her surgical scars Louisa wears a choker made up of several rows of pearls, a visual marker that identifies her with the figure of the Bride of Frankenstein, the separation of whose head from her body is one of her primary characteristics (see Ince 2000: 82–9). If Louisa is Frankenstein's Bride, then Genessier is in a sense also Frankenstein: just as the name circulates between the scientist Victor Frankenstein and his creature in Shelley's novel, monstrous characteristics circulate in Franju's story. Christiane stabs Louisa in the neck, between the strands of pearls in her choker, a direct assault on her identity as a Bride of Frankenstein, and thus her complicity with Genessier's regime.

Louisa's key role in the narrative of *Les Yeux sans visage* supports a reading of patriarchy often made by feminist critics and implicit in Lacan's concept of the Symbolic order, namely, that phallocentric power makes itself felt as violence or loss in all social relationships,

16 'need to dominate'.

including relationships between women. Louisa appears to be and indeed is a kind of substitute mother to Christiane (whose real mother we are never told anything about), but all her kindness to Christiane amounts to is repeated coaxing to wear the mask that makes her appearance socially acceptable, in other words, to collude with Genessier's patriarchal regime. Vital too is that the abductions of young women that supply Genessier with his surgical victims are carried out by Louisa, who is thereby identified as a pure collaborator with patriarchy's crimes. Her final abduction of Paulette Mérodon takes place only after Paulette has been officially discharged from the patriarchal space of medical investigation (it is achieved by Louisa offering her a lift from outside the hospital to the bus stop from which she would return to Paris). Through the person of Louisa, Genessier's criminal activities are entirely mediated by women, hidden from public view and official record, the visible world of patriarchy. And Louisa's feminine gender is an element added by the film's script-writers (Franju, Boileau-Narcejac, Claude Sautet and Jean Redon): in Redon's novel *Celle qui n'était plus* on which *Les Yeux sans visage* is based, the surgeon's assistant is a man, and the surgeon himself is an alcoholic and rather deranged, much more a character of pulp fiction than the sober and chilling Genessier (Chevrie 1986: 46). *Les Yeux sans visage*'s revolutionary family romance is at least in part Franju's invention.

Femininity, madness and freedom

The closing images of *Les Yeux sans visage*, in which Christiane frees white doves from a cage in her father's villa that settle on her shoulder and arm as she glides off past his body into woods, are perhaps the most magical and poetic in the film. Probably because Franju himself suggested that the fluttering doves symbolised her deranged mind, almost everything ever written about the film either does not interpret its final images or agrees that Christiane is mad.[17] In most of these readings it is unclear whether she is supposed to have been this way

17 Even Cowie leaves open this possibility: 'For Christiane, however, there is escape and freedom, although perhaps also madness' (Cowie 2002). Franju said that the final image of the film was romantic but 'l'image même, l'image vraie de la folie' (the true image of madness itself) (Lebovits and Tranchant 1959: 25).

since the accident in which she lost her face, or whether her murder of Louisa and liberation of her father's caged animals (it can be noted that in Genessier's regime human and animal are indistinguishable: an alternative reading of Louisa's neckware to mine suggests that 'The dogs wear studded collars which evoke slavery, while Valli wears a velvet choker, because she is Genessier's dog' (Durgnat 1967: 80)) is the point at which her mind turns. There is, in other words, a dearth of readings of her act of revolt, which I hope to have repaired to some extent above. Even more significant, however, is the fact that by 'diagnosing' madness in Christiane, readings of the end of the film (including Franju's own) have repeated and reinforced the phallocentrism of the main part of its diegesis. Feminist critics of the 1970s, including Hélène Cixous, structured many of their analyses around the observation that in phallogocentric texts – literary, philosophical and other – the opposition of 'male' to female' is homologous to other key binary oppositions such as the opposition of reason to madness. Cixous, Luce Irigaray and Jacques Derrida all concurred about the centrality of oppositional sexual difference to Western thought, and scores of feminist theorists and critics subsequently mined this seam of signification for its riches. An article by Shoshana Felman that was among the first to point out literary criticism's longstanding complicity with phallocentrism focused on the association of madness with femininity in a reading of a Balzac short story (Felman 1975). While the text itself already secondarised femininity, its subsequent abridgement by critics revealed them to be so concerned to eulogise the greatness of Balzacian realism that they were blind both to the phallocentrism of the story's diegesis and to the occlusion of femininity effected by their abridgement.

None of the assumptions of Christiane's madness in *Les Yeux sans visage* link it with other aspects of her character or the rest of the film's narrative, relying instead on the powerful symbolism of the doves seen in its final frames. It is not very controversial to contend that Christiane's behaviour throughout the film gives absolutely no indication of a weak mind, and that there never was a saner gesture of revolt than hers. It can be argued that Christiane is 'mad' to destroy the parent and substitute parent who provide and care for her: since a funeral has been held for her and her fiancé told that she is dead (although he suspects otherwise), there is nowhere left for her to go. In the terms of the Lacanian Symbolic order that is 'understood to precede and orchestrate the parameters of the social' (Butler 1994: 18), she might be claimed to be excluded, since she has no social identity, but if this is the case, it is so throughout her sequestered existence in Genessier's villa. The moment at which Christiane 'goes' mad at the end of *Les Yeux sans visage* cannot be identified, making it a quintessentially open text. I would argue that because of this the doves that have so often been assumed to indicate her madness can just as easily (and just as poetically) symbolise her freedom. Support for this reading can in fact be found in Franju's other films: in *Judex* Jacqueline receives a message in a cage of white pigeons saying that she should free the birds if she is in need of help (which she is, shortly afterwards, upon which one of the pigeons is seen winging its way back to the Château Rouge, Judex's lair by the sea). Here white birds signify freedom and protection, while in the final shot of the film, where Judex repeats his magician's trick from the *bal masqué* of conjuring a white dove out of nothingness, the bird seems associated with love and union. White birds also appear in *La Tête contre les murs*, where the head-to-head conversation between Varmont and Emery about psychiatric methods takes place in front of an aviary Emery is having his patients construct in order to increase their interest in life. These birds are caged rather than free but, unlike Varmont, Emery believes in the concept of an 'asile libre',[18] and shortly beforehand one inmate has been seen carrying uncaged birds towards the aviary, evidently joyful at how they flutter around his hands. The white doves and pigeons that appear across Franju's films might signify many things, but I contend that they should not be read as a privileged signifier of madness in *Les Yeux sans visage*. If there is any madness in the film, it is the same madness of the signifier that Felman unpicked in Balzac's 'Adieu' in 1975, the multivalent polysemy of the white doves that alight on Christiane and flutter around Franju's other fragile, victimised captives.

Eroticism, spirituality and the feminine

The Spanish surrealist director Luis Buñuel figured prominently in the pantheons of his admired directors Franju sometimes enumerated,

18 'open asylum'.

particularly because of the poetic character of his image-making, but also because of its eroticism. Franju's affinity with surrealism extends to the erotic, and while there are very few representations of sex or explicit images of bodies in his cinema, there is certainly an eroticism latent in the charged disjunctures between his images and his fetishism of the human figure and clothing I explored in Chapter 3. (The only erotic relationship of enough narrative importance to lead to sex apart from the paradisiacal coupling of Serge and Albine in *La Faute de l'Abbé Mouret* is the single act of love between François and Stéphanie at the end of *La Tête contre les murs*, just before which François symbolically unfastens the belt of her slacks, an expression of his desperation for freedom.) Franju had very few brushes with censorship in his career, but the most significant was the objection taken by the 'Centrale Catholique du Cinéma' to his representations of the nuns of the order of Saint-Vincent-de-Paul, in *Judex*.[19] Franju refused to make any cuts in response to this organisation's protest about the scene in which Diana Monti/Francine Bergé strips down from her nun's habit to the catsuit she is wearing beneath, whereupon it was reduced to the rather feeble point that during the striptease Bergé had disrespectfully cast her 'cornette' (the symbol of the particular religious order of Saint-Vincent-de-Paul) to the floor (Brumagne 1977: 57). Franju clearly saw no sense in editing out just this part of the striptease, and observed with some pleasure in 1977 that the order had dispensed with the 'cornette' not long after it made its 1963 protest (57).

Fetishism of costume is pronounced in *Judex*, and a certain fetishism of more contemporary clothing comes through in the young people's leathers in *La Tête contre les murs*, and in the shiny black rainwear worn by Louisa/Alida Valli in *Les Yeux sans visage*. (Probably because of other roles she took in Italian and horror cinema that led to her being known just as 'Valli', perversity was an element of Alida Valli's star image: Durgnat calls the way she drags her first female victim's body across rough ground to dispose of it in a weir in *Les Yeux sans visage* 'a perverse embrace: Lesbian, necrophiliac, sadistic' (Durgnat 1967: 80).) Perhaps the most overt moment of perverse sexuality in Franju's cinema, however, occurs in *Pleins feux sur l'assassin*, in the

19 The 'Centrale Catholique du Cinéma' also objected to the dislikeably officious bishop character in *Thomas l'Imposteur*, who refuses to give petrol to the Princesse de Bormes' ambulance convoy until Guillaume/Thomas intervenes.

scene where the authoritative Edwige (Marianne Koch), dressed in a full equestrian outfit after returning from a ride, caresses the groom's thighs with her foot in an attempt to seduce him, wielding her riding crop like a dominatrix as she does so. This moment may be explained by the origins of the story of *Pleins feux sur l'assassin* in popular fiction, but there is no doubt that Franju enjoyed such moments and hints of perversity, since he commented that he would have liked to film Edwige riding accompanied by another beautiful woman, a planned piece of 'sapphisme' with which the film's producers would not indulge him (Gauteur 1970: 78). In other ways too *Pleins feux* works in a more erotic register than any of Franju's other feature films, mainly through the character of Micheline (Dany Saval), the girlfriend of investigating cousin Jean-Marie (Jean-Louis Trintignant). When the couple first arrive at the château anticipating an early funeral for Jean-Marie's uncle, they exchange a deep and lingering kiss before parting for the rest of the day (since Micheline is not 'family', she is not permitted in the château, and the pair only meet up out of hours and out of sight of the building). At a subsequent meeting Micheline swims naked in the castle's lake, although since it is dark nothing explicit is seen. In both visual and narrative terms Micheline occupies the same position of invisibility as Louisa's network of young women in *Les Yeux sans visage*, since although she contributes useful ideas about who the murderer may be to Jean-Marie's detective work, he gives her no credit for these, and reproaches her when she protests about her exclusion from the cousins' activities with 'Tu n'es pas ... présentable!',[20] a classic exclusion of the feminine from language, narrative and sociosymbolic structures.

In *Pleins feux sur l'assassin* the feminine is also associated with modernity. Micheline arrives in rural Brittany from the city, driving a sports car, and finds the entire 'establishment' set-up of Jean-Marie's aristocratic family quaint and amusing. At one point she is impatient enough with her exclusion from even provincial life at the château to tell Jean-Marie that she is returning to Paris, although she actually secretly moves into one of the many empty rooms on the castle's upper floors. Micheline incarnates the kind of free-thinking, disrespectful youthful femininity encapsulated by Brigitte Bardot's Juliette in Roger Vadim's 1956 *Et Dieu créa la femme*, a flagship film for the

20 'You're just not ... presentable!'

nouvelle vague. She is associated with technology and popular culture in the film's final scene, where the Georges Brassens song 'Les Funérailles d'antan' that accompanies the funeral procession is actually intradiegetic music playing on her transistor radio.

Modernity also features in the female characterisation of *Thérèse Desqueyroux*, where Thérèse and Anne de La Trave smoke, ride bicycles and (in Anne's case) shoot for game. Franju's updating of Mauriac's novel from the 1920s to the 1960s is cautious, however, and these activities might equally well have been practised by bourgeois women in the earlier decade. More important in *Thérèse Desqueyroux* is the undercurrent of lesbian attraction that runs from Thérèse to her sister-in-law: Thérèse's intimacy with Anne is one of two reasons she cites for wanting to marry Bernard in the first place. In the first flashback seen while Thérèse travels back from her trial to Argelouse she appears desolate when Anne cycles away home, and her voiceover reflects that she could not get enough of Anne's company in the early days of their friendship.[21] In two subsequent scenes Anne cradles her head on Thérèse's shoulder or on her knee, although it becomes clear from her infatuation with Jean Azévédo that there is nothing sexual in her fondness for Thérèse. Anne speaks of her feelings without embarrassment, saying to Thérèse in the second of these scenes 'Tu m'aimes, toi'.[22] Thérèse, on the other hand, never expresses her feelings directly to Anne, but reacts with obvious jealousy when she receives Anne's letter about Azévédo while on honeymoon in Paris: she will not read the letter until Bernard has gone out, whereupon she runs to scrutinise herself in the bathroom mirror and asks her reflection 'Et moi alors? Moi?'.[23] On her return from the dinner in the Eiffel Tower's restaurant Bernard takes her to that evening she angrily tears up Anne's letter and scatters the pieces from her balcony into the street, thinking to herself that Anne must not find love, that she and Anne must have solitude in common if nothing else. Possessiveness is a feature of Thérèse's character revealed by the bourgeois acquisitiveness that is her second reason for marrying Bernard, but her possessive jealousy is only brought out by Anne, in unspoken and unlived lesbian desire.

21 She was 'insatiable de sa présence'.
22 'You love me, don't you'.
23 'And what about me? Me?'

Conclusion: the whole woman and the fractured man

Like the prominence of the heterosexual family in Franju's features, the undercurrents and moments of perverse and lesbian sexuality in his films indicate a heightened sensitivity to human sexuality and gender. And as my readings of *Judex*, *La Tête contre les murs*, *Thérèse Desqueyroux* and *Les Yeux sans visage* show, the patriarchal family of his features may not appear particularly open to restructuring, but it is certainly not shown to be particularly secure. For his *longs métrages* Franju usually chose narratives that privilege the law-driven, institutional character of the patriarchal family, and if his questioning of it is not as thoroughgoing and corruscating as his critiques of the army and the Church, there are still some suggestive overlaps between the three. The film which offers the best simultaneous critique of two of these institutions is *La Faute de l'Abbé Mouret*, so I shall conclude the chapter with an analysis of how Franju's changes to Zola's novel accomplish this.

A parallel between Franju's anti-clericalism and his questioning of patriarchal structures starts with the nun, the image he most often chose to figure the Church. Priests do appear in Franju's films, but when he wanted simply to allude to institutional religion, as in *Le Sang des bêtes*, *Notre-Dame, cathédrale de Paris* and *La Première Nuit*, it was to nuns that he turned. The brief and semi-arbitrary appearances they make in these three shorts (in no instance are they really linked to narrative action) take on a new significance when compared to the changes to Zola's characterisation Franju made in *La Faute de l'Abbé Mouret*, where he suppresses the character of Serge Mouret's sister Désirée, and significantly alters the characterisation of Albine. As I discussed in Chapter 2, Franju was convinced that Zola had gone 'beyond' his usual naturalism in *La Faute*, and attained an imaginary, *fantastique* dimension, particularly in his descriptions of Le Paradou. It was therefore entirely logical that he should omit the character of Désirée, who is associated throughout the novel with animals and animality (particularly chickens, but also various other farm animals that can be kept on a smallholding). But in so doing Franju strongly modified Zola's conception of femininity, which his *La Faute* associates firmly with the natural world, either animal (Désirée) or vegetable (Albine). In Zola's novel Albine is a 'sauvageonne',[24] who was educated and civilised like a normal girl in her early years, but ran

24 'wild child'.

wild once she arrived at Le Paradou and was taken into Jeanbernat's care. The Albine of Franju's *La Faute* is blonde, laughing and beautiful, but with her smooth skin and straight, glossy hair, has nothing wild about her. By removing femininity's associations with animality and wildness, Franju's adaptation of Zola gives womanhood a newly human status it does not find in Zola's work.

Franju's changes to the plot of Zola's *La Faute* do not only lend humanity to femininity; they increase both its materiality and its spirituality. By making his representations of sex more explicit, both between the peasants Rosalie and Fortuné (a scene not in Zola) and in the coupling of Serge and Albine, where Serge sucks Albine's breast and which Franju described as 'très physique',[25] though also rather confusingly as without 'a hint of eroticism ... very pure' (Beylie 1970: 97), Franju emphasises materialism. But whereas in Zola Serge switches his loyalty from the Virgin Mary to Christ after his idyll with Albine is over, 'Franju's Abbé Mouret never changes his allegiance: for him, Albine and the Virgin are one' (Milne 1970–71: 10). This is affirmed in the closing shots of Franju's film, where Serge gazes at the statue of the Virgin he purchased for his church at his own expense, but sees only the face of Albine, cruelly banished from his life, dead from grief, and buried in consecrated ground only at his insistence. (In Zola Serge returns to Le Paradou to discover that his love for Albine is no more, but in Franju Albine visits his church herself only to be ejected, after which she seeks out a death from asphyxiation by flowers she has picked in their Garden of Eden.) Albine is both a dreamy, golden fantasy (her eyes are at first half-closed in ecstasy as Serge kisses her cheek and then her mouth in the shots of her that end the film) and a woman of flesh and blood. She is the Virgin Mary and an Eve figure: the traditional phallocentric split between spiritual and sexual femininity ('virgin' and 'whore') is repaired by Franju's modifications to Zola's characterisation and narrative. Important too is that on her second appearance in Franju's film Albine is dressed entirely in white and wearing a leafy crown that bears more than a casual resemblance to Christ's crown of thorns. This brings her into intratextual contact with Christiane in *Les Yeux sans visage*, whose name suggests a Christ-like status in relation to her God-like father ('"Genessier" sounds like "Genesis"' (Durgnat 1967: 86)). Like Christ,

25 'very physical'.

Albine suffers and is extinguished for her power (the threat she represents to Serge's place in the priesthood), the difference being that in *La Faute* power is coded as female and erotic/sexual.

One further modification Franju made to Zola's *La Faute de l'Abbé Mouret* confirms his transformation of Zola's representation of femininity – the addition of the character of Mère Corentin, an old woman who is seen 'on her death-bed, eyes staring and jaw gaping in a flutter of feathers from her pillaged mattress' (Milne 1970–71: 11). First, the invention of Mère Corentin, like the omission of Désirée, shifts the balance of female characters from a predominantly young, simple-minded and naïve set of women in Zola's novel to an older and wiser, more authoritative cast. Second, the shot of Mère Corentin on her death-bed takes up a place in a remarkable sequence of three shots of supine women that is entirely Franju's creation – the statue of the Virgin on her bed of straw, Mère Corentin ministered to by Mouret but surrounded by her scavenging relatives, and Albine on her bed of flowers, gently drifting into death. A young and an old woman, and the Virgin Mary, femininity in all its guises, thwarted but with its own mysterious force – the statue of the Virgin rises from her packing case apparently unaided by Serge, who smiles broadly at the equal height this surrection (resurrection? insurrection?) has bestowed upon her figure. This scene furthers my discussion in Chapter 3 of how Franju's camerawork animates the human figure, and, as Claude Beylie notes, is a remarkably suggestive piece of filming, which expresses all the notions Franju's film conveys 'de surgissement de la sensualité, de réveil physique, d'irrésistible épanouissement vital' (Beylie 1970: 100).[26]

An element of fantasy subsists in this 'ascension' of the Virgin Mary, and this is repeated at the end of *La Faute* when Serge raises his arms and face towards the altar-mounted statue, surrounded by flowers just like the lilies chosen by Albine for her death-bed. Albine now appears to him, 'resurrected' as a beautiful and amorous woman: she lives on in the religious fantasies which in Franju's version of Zola are inextricable from sexual ones. What these eruptions of fantasy into the narrative of *La Faute de l'Abbé Mouret* indicate is the incompleteness of male subjectivity – a subjectivity that constantly strives for completion and satisfaction, but in Serge's case is only found in his brief idyll with Albine. Most of Franju's male characters are closer

26 'of sensuality rising up, of physical awakening, of an irresistible blossoming of life'.

to the stereotype of the patriarch than to this fractured, fantasising kind of masculinity: the protagonist who most resembles Serge Mouret is François Gérane,[27] whose one act of love with Stéphanie (his only respite from his form of institutional confinement, both in the asylum and outside it) marks a moment of freedom he is not mature enough to hold on to or trust. François's struggle is for an adult masculinity his upbringing has prevented him from attaining, which we see him trying (in vain) to achieve alone: Serge Mouret's double 'marriage' to the Church and to Albine brings masculinity's division between institutional loyalty and sexual love into much bleaker focus. But in their respective ways both Serge and François represent a different kind of masculinity to the patriarchal stereotype at the head of Franju's oppressive families, one revelatory of another – and more promising – regime of sexual subjectivities. *Judex* is the only one of Franju's films to have a romantically happy conclusion, but men like François and Serge, whose family-related personal and spiritual con-flicts prevent them finding lasting happiness, do recognise women (in Serge's case unconsciously) as equal, separate and sexual subjects.

The repeated suggestion of equal male–female relationships made in Franju's films is a rarity in French cinema of the 1950s and 1960s, but entirely consistent with Franju's personal views on social inequi-ties, and with the protest against society's victimising institutions implied in the audaciousness of his early *courts métrages* and his ques-tioning of the patriarchal family. To call his vision of sexual subjecti-vities and relations 'feminist' would probably be overstating the case, and rather anachronistic in view of the emergent state of second-wave feminism in 1960s France. If the vision is humanist, it is still, as Robert Brown points out, 'altogether too facile to equate Franju's anti-institutionalism with his humanism' (Brown 1983: 269). The sexual equality glimpsed in Franju's fictions is not the kind that exists between the freely interrelating subjectivities of liberal political theory. (Since they contain a preponderance of female protagonists, a liberal Enlighten-ment-based model of womanhood would imply a politically balanced fictional universe featuring powerful women and matriarchs, when these do not in fact figure in it at all.) Franju's vision of a gendered society includes fragile and criminal women as well as female pioneers and women of revolutionary courage, and highly sympathetic immature

27 Judex and Thomas share some of its hesitancy and dependency on femininity.

and conflict-ridden men. For him, masculine fantasy and feminine melodrama are products of the incompleteness of subjectivity that follows from symbolic sexual existence, a non-phallocentric Symbolic order more symmetrical than the Lacanian one, and an order that relations with the other sex or gender help to found. Franju's anti-institutionalist attitude takes account of the violences wrought by society on women, men and all unfree beings, and envisions sexuality and its accompanying fantasies and emotional life as a fracturing of subjectivity that sustains human desire even as it impedes it.

References

Beylie, Claude (1970), 'Franju entre Zola et Roy Vickers', *Cinéma* 150 (November), 93–105.

Borde, Raymond (1962), 'Pari sur "Thérèse Desqueyroux"', *Positif* 47 (July), 61–3.

Bowman, Curtis (2002), 'A film without politics: Georges Franju's *Les Yeux sans visage*', *Kinoeye: New Perspectives on European Film* 2(13) (9 September). Available online at www.kinoeye.org/02/13/bowman13.php. Accessed 8 September 2004.

Brown, Robert (1983), 'Georges Franju: behind closed windows', *Sight and Sound* 52: 4 (autumn), 266–71.

Brumagne, Marie-Madeleine (1977), *Georges Franju. Impressions et aveux*, Lausanne, l'Age d'Homme.

Butler, Judith (1994), 'Against proper objects', *differences* 6(2–3), 1–26.

Chevassu, François (1988), 'Franju l'insolite', *La Revue du cinéma* 434 (January), 67–77.

Chevrie, Marc (1986), 'Les figures de la peur' (interview), *Cahiers du cinéma* 389 (November), 45–7.

Cowie, Elizabeth (2002), 'Anxiety, ethics and horror: Georges Franju's *Les Yeux sans visage*', *Kinoeye: New Perspectives on European Film* 2(13) (9 September). Available online at www.kinoeye.org/02/13/cowie13.php. Accessed 8 September 2004.

Durgnat, Raymond (1967), *Franju*, London, Studio Vista.

Felman, Shoshana (1975), 'Woman and madness: the critical phallacy', *Diacritics* 5(4) (winter), 2–10.

Gauteur, Claude (1970), 'Georges Franju' (interview), *Image et Son* 245 (December), 76–80.

Hawkins, Joan (2000), *Cutting Edge. Art Horror and the Horrific Avant-Garde*, Minneapolis and London, University of Minnesota Press.

Ince, Kate (2000), *Orlan: Millennial Female*, Oxford and New York, Berg.

Lebovits, Jean-Marc and Tranchant, François (1959), 'Entretien avec Georges Franju cinéaste et poète du merveilleux quotidien', *Cinéma* 34 (March), 16–25.

Milne, Tom (1970–71), 'Songs of innocence', *Sight and Sound* 40(1) (winter), 7–11.

Conclusion

Franju was an 'enfant de la salle obscure'[1] (Beylie 1987a) who went on to devote his adult life to French cinema. He never left France except to do compulsory military service in Algeria before the Second World War, and refused a world tour to talk about his films and his profession offered to him in the 1970s (Brumagne 1977: 72). A lifelong attachment to the cinema of Murnau, Lang, Renoir and Buñuel reveals both his immersion in the values of classic cinema and a taste for modernist invention. He remained nostalgic for the age of silent cinema and the time when black and white reigned supreme, because silence allowed images to do the talking, and black and white film allowed one to 'joue[r] avec les valeurs' (Brumagne 1977: 59).[2] To an extent, he lived in an imaginary realm: his earliest memories were of striking, disjunctive 'insolite' images. As a quotation Marc Chevrie uses in his 1986 interview explains, 'Franju n'a pas d'idées, il a des visions' (Chevrie 1986: 45).[3] In summarising the contribution his singular voice made to French cinema, it is hard to improve on the homage paid by Henri Langlois on the twentieth anniversary of the Cinémathèque française in 1956 and reprinted in an obituary by Claude Beylie:

> "Révolutionnaire malgré lui, pamphlétaire sans le savoir [...] Georges Franju se promène avec la grandeur du garnement du conte d'Andersen qui voyait bien que le roi était nu, et ne se gênait pas pour le dire. C'est pourquoi il est le seul metteur en scène insolite de ce temps; et le seul, depuis Vigo, à soumettre l'objectif à sa vision, à lui ôter toute

1 'a dark-room child'.
2 'play with values'.
3 'Franju doesn't have ideas, he has visions'.

participation involontaire". C'était cela, en effet, Georges Franju: un sens très pur de la révolte, une vive ingénuité créatrice, un mépris souverain des conventions, l'orgueil mêlé d'humilité des grands rebelles, le goût du mystère tapi au coeur du quotidien. Autant de dispositions naturelles – rares – qui ont irrigué toute son oeuvre.[4] (Beylie 1987b)

In my introduction to this book, I suggested that the contribution made to French and international cinema by Franju's idiomatic voice has usually been badly understood and insufficiently appreciated, although for reasons that are comprehensible and traceable. Now that I have discussed the films themselves under headings designed to shed new light upon his work (this applies particularly to Chapters 2 and 4), I would like to return to the paradox of his marginal status within French cinema. It is a status of which Franju himself was aware: when asked after 1974 why he was no longer making films, he joked that it was because he had stopped trying to keep up contacts with producers, and consequently wasn't getting any offers: 'Vous savez, je n'ai jamais été moi, dans le courant cinématographique ... Je ne suis pas du tout du cinéma de 36, comme on l'a dit et je ne suis pas non plus du tout de la Nouvelle Vague ... C'est Jeanson qui disait: il y en a qui disent que Franju est un metteur en scène d'avant-guerre ... Oui, la prochaine!'[5] Franju was both right 'inside' French cinema – dubbed the greatest French director by *Positif* early in his career and widely known as a cinephile's *cinéaste* – and 'outside' it, in the sense that his place in it was never clear or enduringly secure. In so far as he was for many years solely a director of *court métrage*, this makes sense: even in an age when short films enjoyed far more respectability as an art form

---

4 '"A revolutionary in spite of himself and a lampoonist unaware of his satirical talent, Georges Franju has the greatness of the boy in Andersen's tale who could see the emperor had no clothes on, and wasn't afraid to say so. This is why he is the only 'insolite' director of our time, and the only one since Vigo to make the camera's lens express his vision, and only his vision". That was, indeed, Georges Franju: a very pure sense of revolt, a lively creative imagination, a sovereign disregard for convention, the mixture of pride and humility only great rebels have, and a taste for mystery at the heart of the everyday. A set of natural – and rare – abilities that pervade his entire oeuvre'.

5 'I've never been fashionable in cinema, you know ... I'm not part of 1930s cinema as some people have suggested, and I'm not part of the New Wave at all either ... As Jeanson put it: some people say that Franju is a pre-war director ... Yes, the next war!'

than they have done at any time since, *Le Sang des bêtes* had no commercial release outside Paris, *Hôtel des Invalides* was distributed on a programme with *Le Trou normand*, a Bourvil comedy, and *Le Grand Méliès* was paired with a Walt Disney film (Garcia 1954: 7). But as I have emphasised throughout my chapters, the 'Franju enigma' has as much to do with the way his films have been received by critics and historians as with their popularity (or lack of it) with audiences.

The variety of terms I have already used to describe Franju's marginality – a displacement in history, a 'singular' or 'idiomatic' voice, the 'paradox' of simultaneous inclusion and exclusion, the 'Franju enigma' – is itself an illustration of the inadequacy of critical concepts developed to discuss his cinema (Leblanc 1996a: 59). Like Gérard Leblanc, I find 'realism' inappropriate and the *fantastique* nothing but an operator of closure when used as a genre label (Leblanc 1996a: 63). As Leblanc states, the 'official' surrealist definition of the 'insolite' as 'the admixture of the natural and the supernatural in a single object' (61) has not been able to generate any adequate critical model. But although Leblanc concludes his first essay of 1996 by saying that Franju's 'démarche'[6] is as difficult to analyse today as it has always been, because it is poetic in the sense that it results from 'the explosive confrontation between the apparently rational explanation of given reality and what the film-maker has felt and understood of that reality' (68), his second essay of the same year (1996b) goes some way to filling this conceptual lacuna. The notions on which he draws to do this are the 'entre-deux' and 'indétermination',[7] both of which describe a non-resolution of the dialectical tension between opposites, particularly 'subject' and 'object' (1996b: 87), and the way Franju's filming of objects tears them away from existing contextual determinations and renders them indeterminate (88). These two essays, where Leblanc extends the analyses conducted in his 1992 book *Une esthétique de la déstabilisation*, focus solely on the *courts métrages*, but in my view 'indeterminacy', in particular, is a helpful concept to employ when looking at the entirety of Franju's oeuvre.

The first chapter of this study demonstrated, I hope, that much and perhaps the greater part of Franju's most powerful work lies in *court métrage*, always cinema's 'minor' format (to use a Deleuzian

6 'procedure'.
7 'between-two' and 'indeterminacy'.

term). When the incommensurability of *court* and *long métrage* is considered, Franju's authorship of a substantial corpus of films in both formats (which according to him may not require different work-ing methods, but which certainly have distinct histories, audiences and methods of distribution), gives his oeuvre an indeterminacy: it is a divided body of work, one with an unstable identity. The critical framework I employed in Chapter 2 was formulated in order to show that Franju's feature films have a questioning, uncertain and plural relationship to cinematic genre: *cinéma fantastique* is an inadequate and misleading single label to apply to them. (Interestingly, by late in his life Franju was himself expressing irritation with the reception of his features as *cinéma fantastique*, which he described as 'de l'esbroufe, de la camelote, du tape-à-l'oeil, de la foutaise, du toc!' (Maison de la Villette 1992: 100).[8]) In Chapter 3 instability and indeterminacy were revealed at work not only in the relationship Franju's cinema sets up with the real (the known is more horror-inspiring than the unknown; exterior locations are given the same composite complexity as studio sets) but within the frame itself. Franju was a film-maker of *mise-en-scène* rather than of *montage*, but this does not imply any lack of movement in his images: the dynamism of his film-making arises within each shot, in his interrogation of the contents of the frame, the 'dialectical movement within the shot' first observed by Buache in the 1950s (Buache 1955: 35). In Chapter 4, I uncovered a Franju parti-cularly alive to the play of difference in personal identity: just like the 'tremblement' between his films and genre categories described by Matthieu Lindon in *Libération* that I quoted at the end of Chapter 2, gender identities and subjectivities in Franju's narratives are unstable and fractured. Finally, the pattern of indeterminacy – of difference(s) resisting containment within identity – can also be seen in Franju's relationship to the commissioning of his films: the limits established by 'commandes' gave him a discipline within which to work, but the film always evolved within these parameters and ended up over-flowing the frame (Vialle 1968: 89).

I also suggested in my readings of gender identity and narrative in Chapter 4 that while psychoanalytic insights about subjectivity and sexuality are definitely of value to Franju criticism, his films resist the hermetic, predictable and phallocentric frameworks on which psycho-

8 'hot air, rubbish, for show, bullshit, fake'.

analytic criticism has often relied – Freud's Oedipalism and Lacan's concept of the Symbolic order. In this context, it should perhaps not be forgotten that Franju was a lifelong depressive who regarded psychoanalysis as an art rather than a science (70). However, it was not analysis he depended on to keep him going, but his work: 'if I don't work I'm down and if I do I'm up' (70); film-making was his *raison d'être* and the 'thérapeutique-miracle'[9] that protected him from his chronic states of depressive anxiety (Brumagne 1977: 19). If I choose to end this book by mentioning this biographical information, it is to keep a place for psychoanalysis in a study in which I have not employed it much, and to sound a reminder that Freudian and Lacanian insights can tell us as much about artists and how they work as about film, painting or literature. In the understanding of Franju I have developed while writing this study I may be guilty of psycho-analysing him, but if this is the case it is because of an identification with his way of working and of seeing the world. I hope I will be indulged for insisting that psychoanalysis is of relevance to Franju, because it can help us understand a film artist's relationship to his cinema that was one of therapy rather than symptom.

9 'miracle therapy'.

References

Beylie, Claude (1987a), 'Tombeau de Georges Franju', *Cinéma* 415 (November), 30.

Beylie, Claude (1987b), 'Georges Franju' (obituary), *L'Avant-Scène Cinéma* 366 (December), 89.

Brumagne, Marie-Madeleine (1977), *Georges Franju. Impressions et aveux*, Lausanne, l'Age d'Homme.

Buache, Freddy (1955), 'Les premiers films de Georges Franju', *Positif* 13 (March–April), 33–5.

Chevrie, Marc (1986), 'Les figures de la peur' (interview), *Cahiers du cinéma* 389 (November), 45–7.

Garcia, Pierre (1954), 'Un poète émotif: Georges Franju', *Image et Son* 72 (May), 7–8.

Leblanc, Gérard (1992), *Une esthétique de la déstabilisation*, Paris, Maison de la Villette.

Leblanc, Gérard (1996a), 'La réception critique du cinéma de Georges Franju', in Daniel Serceau (sous la direction de), *Le Cinéma. L'Après-guerre et le réalisme*, Paris, Editions Jean-Michel Place, pp. 59–68.

Leblanc, Gérard (1996b), 'L'entre-deux: à propos du cinéma de Georges Franju', in Daniel Serceau (sous la direction de), *Le Cinéma. L'Après-guerre et le réalisme*, Paris, Editions Jean-Michel Place, pp. 83–92.

Maison de la Villette (1992), *Georges Franju cinéaste*, Paris, Maison de la Villette.

Milne, Tom (1975),'Georges Franju: The Haunted Void', *Sight and Sound* 44(2) (spring), 68–72.

Vialle, Gabriel (1968), *Georges Franju*, Paris, Seghers.

Filmography

Films are listed by the date shooting was completed, with the release date in Paris given in brackets for the *longs métrages*.

Courts métrages

Le Métro (1935) 8 mins, b/w, silent. Co-directed with Henri Langlois
Screenplay: Georges Franju and Henri Langlois

Le Sang des bêtes (1948) 21 mins, b/w

Production company: Forces et Voix de France
Screenplay: Georges Franju
Photography: Marcel Fradetal
Music: Joseph Kosma
Commentary: Jean Painlevé, spoken by Nicole Ladmiral and Georges Hubert

En passant par la Lorraine (1950) 31 mins, b/w

Production company: Forces et Voix de France
Screenplay: Georges Franju
Photography: Marcel Fradetal
Music: Joseph Kosma
Commentary: Georges Franju, spoken by Georges Hubert

Hôtel des Invalides (1951) 22 mins, b/w

Production company: Forces et Voix de France

Screenplay: Georges Franju
Photography: Marcel Fradetal
Music: Maurice Jarre
Commentary: Georges Franju and war museum's own, spoken by Michel Simon and museum guides Bordène and Rusé

Le Grand Méliès (1952) 30 mins, b/w

Production company: Armor Films
Screenplay: Georges Franju
Photography: Jacques Mercanton
Music: Georges Van Parys
Art Direction: Henri Schmitt
Commentary: Georges Franju, spoken by Mme Marie-Georges Méliès and Marcel Lallemant
Actors: Mme Marie-Georges Méliès (herself), André Méliès (himself and Georges Méliès)

Monsieur et Madame Curie (1953) 14 mins, b/w

Production company: Téléfilm, Armor Films
Screenplay: Georges Franju, based on Marie Curie's *Pierre Curie*
Photography: Jacques Mercanton
Music: Beethoven (*Les Adieux* piano sonata)
Commentary: Based on Marie Curie's *Pierre Curie*, spoken by Nicole Stéphane
Actors: Nicole Stéphane (Marie Curie), Lucien Hubert (Pierre Curie)

Les Poussières (1954) 22 mins, b/w

Production company: Armor Films
Screenplay: Georges Franju
Photography: Jacques Mercanton
Music: Jean Wiener
Commentary: Georges Franju, spoken by Georges Hubert

[Navigation marchande (1954). Film renounced by Franju.]

A propos d'une rivière (1955) 25 mins, b/w

Production company: Procinex
Screenplay: Michel Duborgel and Georges Franju

Photography: Quinto Albicocco
Music: Henri Crolla
Sound: André Hodeir
Commentary: Michel Duborgel and Georges Franju, spoken by Marcel and Jean-Paul Laporte
Actors: Michel Duborgel (the fisherman)

Mon chien (1955) 19 mins, b/w

Production company: Procinex, Ancinex
Screenplay: Georges Franju
Photography: Georges Delaunay and Jean Penzer
Music: Henri Crolla
Commentary: Jacques Prévert, spoken by Roger Pigaut
Actors: Jacqueline Lemaire (the girl)

Le Théâtre national populaire (1956) 28 mins, b/w

Production company: Procinex, Ancinex
Screenplay: Georges Franju
Photography: Marcel Fradetal
Music: Maurice Jarre
Commentary: Georges Franju, spoken by Marc Cassot
Actors: Jean Vilar, Maria Casarès, Gérard Philippe, Silvia Montfort, Georges Wilson, Daniel Sorano, Monique Chaumette, Jean Topart

Sur le pont d'Avignon (1956) 11 mins, col

Production company: Procinex, Ancinex
Screenplay: Georges Franju
Photography: Marcel Fradetal
Music: Maurice Jarre
Commentary: Georges Franju, spoken by Claude Dasset

Notre-Dame, cathédrale de Paris (1957) 13 mins, col

Production company: Argos Films
Screenplay: Georges Franju
Photography: Marcel Fradetal
Music: Jean Wiener
Commentary: Frédéric de Towarnicki, spoken by Muriel Chaney

La Première Nuit (1958) 18 mins, b/w

Production company: Argos Films
Screenplay: Marianne Oswald and Remo Forlani
Adaptation: Georges Franju
Photography: Eugen Shuftan
Music: Georges Delerue
Actors: Pierre Devis, Lisbeth Person

Longs métrages

La Tête contre les murs (1958) (release 20 March 1959), 100 mins, b/w

Production company: Atica, Sinus, Elphenor
Screenplay: Jean-Pierre Mocky
Photography: Eugen Shuftan
Sound: René Sarazin
Music: Maurice Jarre
Editing: Suzanne Sandberg
Actors: Jean-Pierre Mocky (François Gérane), Anouk Aimée (Stéphanie), Pierre Brasseur (docteur Varmont), Paul Meurisse (docteur Emery), Charles Aznavour (Heurtevent), Jean Galland (maître Gérane), Jean Ozeunne (comte de Chambrelle), Thomy Bourdelle (colonel Donadieu), Rudy Lenoir (le planqué), Luis Masson (l'interne), Edith Scob (la jeune folle)

Les Yeux sans visage (1959) (release 2 March 1960), 90 mins, b/w

Production company: Champs-Elysées Productions, Lux Films
Screenplay: Jean Redon
Adaptation: Jean Redon, Georges Franju, Claude Sautet, Pierre Boileau-Thomas Narcejac
Photography: Eugen Shuftan
Sound: Antoine Archambaud
Music: Maurice Jarre
Editing: Gilbert Natot
Actors: Edith Scob (Christiane Genessier), Pierre Brasseur (docteur Genessier), Alida Valli (Louise), Juliette Mayniel (Edna), Béatrice Altariba (Paulette), François Guérin (Jacques), René Génin (Tessot), Michel Etchevéry (le médecin légiste), Alexandra Rignault et Claude Brasseur (les inspecteurs de police), Marcel Pérès et Charles Blavette (les hommes dans le cimetière), Charles Blavette (l'employé de la fourrière), Birgitta Juslin (la copine d'Edna), Yvette Etievant (la mère du petit malade)

Pleins feux sur l'assassin (1960) (release 31 March 1961), 88 mins, b/w

Production company: Champs-Elysées Productions (Jules Borkon)
Screenplay: Pierre Boileau-Thomas Narcejac
Photography: Marcel Fradetal
Sound: Robert Biart
Music: Maurice Jarre
Editing: Gilbert Natot
Actors: Pierre Brasseur (comte de Keraudren), Jean-Louis Trintignant (Jean-Marie), Dany Saval (Micheline), Pascale Audret (Jeanne), Jean Babilée (Christian), Marianne Koch (Edwige), Philippe Leroy-Beaulieu (André), Jean Ozenne (Guillaume), Gérard Buhr, Georges Rolin, Serge Marquand, Maryse Martin, Lucien Raimbourg, Robert Vattier

Thérèse Desqueyroux (1962) (release 21 September 1962), 109 mins, b/w

Production company: Filmel (Eugène Lépicier)
Screenplay: François Mauriac, Claude Mauriac, Georges Franju (from François Mauriac's novel)
Photography: Christian Matras
Sound: Jacques Labussière
Music: Maurice Jarre
Editing: Gilbert Natot
Actors: Emmanuèle Riva (Thérèse Desqueyroux), Philippe Noiret (Bernard Desqueyroux), Edith Scob (Anne de La Trave), Sami Frey (Jean Azévédo), Renée Devillers (Mme de La Trave), Richard Saint-Bris (M. de La Trave), Lucien Nat (Laroque), Hélène Dieudonné (tante Clara), Jeanne Perez (Balionte), Jacques Monod (maître Duros)

Judex (1963) (release 4 December 1963), 103 mins, b/w

Production company: Comptoir français du film, Films Rome
Screenplay: Jacques Champreux, Francis Lacassin, based on Arthur Bernède and Louis Feuillade's *Judex*
Photography: Marcel Fradetal
Sound: Jean Labussière
Music: Maurice Jarre
Editing: Gilbert Natot
Actors: Channing Pollock (Judex, Vallières), Edith Scob (Jacqueline Favraux), Francine Bergé (Marie Verdier, Diana Monti), Théo Sarapo (Moralès), René Génin (Kerjean), Syvia Koscina (Daisy), Benjamin Boda (Réglisse)

Thomas l'imposteur (1965) (release 3 May 1965), 100 mins, b/w

Production company: Filmel (Eugène Lépicier)
Screenplay: Jean Cocteau, Michel Worms, Georges Franju (from Jean Cocteau's novel)
Photography: Marcel Fradetal
Sound: André Hervé, Raymond Gaugier
Music: Georges Auric
Editing: Gilbert Natot
Actors: Emmanuèle Riva (Princesse de Bormes), Fabrice Rouleau (Thomas), Sophie Darès (Henriette de Bormes), Jean Servais (Pesquel-Duport), Rosy Varte (Mme Valiche), Michel Vitold (docteur Verne), Bernard Lavalette (docteur Gentil), Edouard Dhermite (capitaine Roy), Hélène Dieudonné (Mlle Thomas), Jean-Roger Caussimon (l'évêque)

La Faute de l'Abbé Mouret (1970) (release 14 October 1970), 100 mins, col

Production company: Stephan-Films, Films du Carrosse, Valoria Films, New Films Productions
Screenplay: Jean Ferry, Georges Franju (from Emile Zola's novel)
Photography: Marcel Fradetal
Sound: Bernard Aubouy
Music: Jean Wiener
Editing: Gilbert Natot
Actors: Francis Huster (l'abbé Mouret), Gillian Hills (Albine), André Lacombe (frère Archangias), Margo Lion (La Teuse), Hugo-Fausto Tozzi (Jeanbernat), Tino Carraro (docteur Pascal), Lucien Barjon (Bambousse), Sylvie Feit (Rosalie)

Nuits rouges (1973) (release 20 November 1974), 105 mins, col

Production company: Terre-Film, S.O.A.T
Screenplay: Jacques Champreux
Photography: Ronzo Bertoni, Robert Foncard
Sound and Music ('Illustration sonore'): Georges Franju
Editing: Gilbert Natot
Actors: Jacques Champreux (l'homme), Gayle Hunnicutt (la femme), Gert Froebe (commissaire Scorbier), Patrick Préjean (Séraphin), Joséphine Chaplin (Martine), Clément Harari (docteur Dutreuil), Hugo Pagliai (Paul), Raymond Bussières (l'acheteur), Pierre Collet (le Grand Maître des Templiers), Henri Lincoln (professeur Petrie), Yvon Sarray (Albert), Enzo Fisichella (inspecteur Peclet), Gérard Croce (La Futaille), Jean Saudray (le sacristain), Michel Paulin (inspecteur Florent), André Jaud (inspecteur Lenfant)

Select bibliography

See also the lists of references at the end of each chapter.

Books

Brumagne, Marie-Madeleine (1977), *Georges Franju. Impressions et aveux*, Lausanne, l'Age d'Homme, 135pp. A very useful book of conversations that works through Franju's films in chronological order from the earliest *courts métrages* up to his last feature film, and often touches on biographical, historical and aesthetic issues. Also contains Franju's script, adaptation and dialogues for the unmade project *La Princesse et le comédien*, from E.T.A. Hoffmann's *Princess Bambilla*.

Buache, Freddy (1996), *Georges Franju: poésie et vérité*, Paris, Cinémathèque française, 75pp. The first part of this book is a reissued version of the text on Franju Buache published in 1959 in *Premier Plan* 1, while the rest contains previously unpublished responses to all Franju's feature films from *Les Yeux sans visage* on, as well as to the three full-length films he made for television (*La Ligne d'Ombre*, *La Discorde* and *Le Dernier Mélodrame*) and one short made for German television and scripted by Marguerite Duras (*Les Rideaux blancs*). It also includes some of the best, beautifully reproduced photograms from many of Franju's films.

Durgnat, Raymond (1967), *Franju*, London, Studio Vista, 144pp. The only thorough account of Franju's cinema in English to date, this book contains a valuable introductory section on Franju's style and aesthetics ('The Artist'), and sections of generous length on all the *courts métrages* and the feature films up to *Thomas l'Imposteur*. Durgnat's approach and insights are idiosyncratic but often highly rewarding.

Leblanc, Gérard (1992), *Une esthétique de la déstabilisation*, Paris, Maison de la Villette, 112pp. Leblanc is the only French academic to have 'revisited' Franju's films with new critical insights since the film-maker's death in 1987, and although his book is far from a complete study, it contains illuminating analyses of Franju's aesthetics and many high-quality stills from the films.

Maison de la Villette (1992), *Georges Franju cinéaste*, Paris, Maison de la Villette, 163pp. Published alongside Leblanc's monograph in tandem with a major exhibition on Franju mounted by the Maison de la Villette in 1992, this volume contains some previously unpublished Franju typescripts from the archives of the Cinémathèque française, and a number of absorbing articles by Franju's collaborators, critics and friends, including Georges-Patrick Langlois, Jacques Champreux and Edith Scob.

Vialle, Gabriel (1968), *Georges Franju*, Paris, Seghers, 191pp. The first serious book published on Franju in French after Freddy Buache's 1959 monograph in *Premier Plan*, this contains a lot of useful material, including extracts of previously unpublished writings by Franju. Its critical purview is limited by Vialle's insistence on categorising Franju as a surrealist.

Articles and interviews

Brown, Robert, 'Georges Franju: behind closed windows', *Sight and Sound* 52(4) (autumn 1983), 266–71.

Buache, Freddy, 'Les Premiers Films de Georges Franju', *Positif* 13 (March–April 1955), 33–5.

Buache, Freddy, 'Entretien avec Georges Franju', *Positif* 25–6 (autumn 1957), 13–21.

Bureau, Patrick, 'Entretien avec Georges Franju', *Contre-champ* 4 (October 1962), 5–8.

Daney, Serge, 'L'Oeil était dans la tombe et regardait Franju', *Libération* 25 September 1986.

Demeure, Jacques, and Kyrou, Ado, 'Le Plus Grand Cinéaste Français [*sic*]', *Positif* 16 (May 1956), 37–40.

Fieschi, Jean-André and Labarthe, André S., 'Nouvel entretien avec Georges Franju', *Cahiers du cinéma* 149 (November 1963), 1–17.

Image et Son 192 (March 1966), special issue on Franju.

Leblanc, Gérard, 'La réception critique du cinéma de Georges Franju', in Daniel Serceau (sous la direction de), *Le Cinéma. L'Après-guerre et le réalisme*, Paris, Editions Jean-Michel Place, 1996, pp. 59–68.

Leblanc, Gérard, 'L'entre-deux: à propos du cinéma de Georges Franju', in Daniel Serceau (sous la direction de), *Le Cinéma. L'Après-guerre et le réalisme*, Paris, Editions Jean-Michel Place, 1996, pp. 83–92.

Milne, Tom, 'Georges Franju: the haunted void', *Sight and Sound* 44(2) (spring 1975), 68–72.

Truffaut, François, 'Entretien avec Georges Franju', *Cahiers du cinéma* 101 (November 1959), 1–15.

Index

Page numbers in italics refer to illustrations while 'n'. after a page reference indicates the number of a note on that page.